Droog D

Design
Spirit of the Nineties

edited by Renny Ramakers and Gijs Bakker

introduction by Paola Antonelli

010 Publishers, Rotterdam 1998

Conten

ts

Foreword

This book represents a continuing journey. An overview of five years of Droog Design. Our debut came in the spring of 1993 during the International Furniture Fair in Milan with a modest show of offbeat items by young Dutch designers. We evidently came at the right time, for the response was overwhelming.

Now, five years on, we have gathered together a wide range of products under the name 'Droog Design'. These we either choose from the latest supply or initiate by setting up projects.

Some items in the Droog collection have the air of a manifesto, others are somewhat less outspoken. The one product is so complex or experimental that it is destined to remain at the prototype stage; the other is being produced in series. Our criteria are flexible, shaped as they are by developments in product culture and by whatever direction designers are heading in. The only constant is that the concept has validity today and that it is worked out along lines that are clear-cut and compelling. Within this framework, literally anything goes. And the focus is steadily shifting. At our first show it was simple, readily available materials that prevailed - wrapping paper, rags and the like. A few years later we were exhibiting products made from synthetic materials. And now decoration, it seems, is a subject of serious concern.

We choose our products regardless of their potential for industrial production and market success. Not that we rule out that possibility - far from it. Logging into the reality of demand and supply is of inestimable importance. Without it there is a real danger of isolation. Thanks to the untiring commitment of a handful of progressive young companies - in particular DMD and the international network this Dutch firm has built up - Droog Design has moved into a front-line position in the market.

These days, international firms are becoming aware of our existence. They come to us with commissions, as much for experimental projects as for realistic product development. We regard this as an important expansion of our activities. Such commissions stimulate the interaction between creative design work and the reality of production and market. The Droog collection emanates the 'spirit of the nineties'. Not by being part of the dominant culture, but because our products challenge that culture, run counter to it - in other words, derive their recalcitrance from it. We certainly don't see them as the definitive solution to a problem or the one direction to take but as the door to any number of possibilities. Only the future can tell what the ultimate impact of Droog Design will be. How Droog will continue to develop in the coming years depends on the designers. The first move, after all, will always be theirs.

Renny Ramakers

Nothing
than Dry

Cooler

by Paola Antonelli

Nothing Cooler than Dry

Paola Antonelli

Five years ago, Droog Design arrived as a subtle, yet powerful, sign of the times which everyone in the design community immediately recognized and acknowledged. It was a seemingly casual gathering of things and personalities whose names all non-Dutch people had a hard time pronouncing. Among the first objects that Droog's initiators Renny Ramakers and Gijs Bakker presented were a series of what appeared to be design accidents, like Tejo Remy's accumulation of drawers without a cabinet and his 'Rag Chair' - both held together by belts. Not your typical user-friendly designs. The message was unspoken, yet clear, and the universal success granted to Droog has been based not only on the smart beauty and negligent elegance of its individual objects but also on the appropriateness of the collection as a whole.

After a show in February 1993 organized by Renny Ramakers on the first floor of the Amsterdam rock club Paradiso, Ramakers and Bakker staged Droog's first international appearance, at the Salone del Mobile, the furniture fair of Milan, in April 1993. The Salone is a peculiar trade show which has more in common with an art fair or the Cannes Film Festival than with a machine-parts salespeople's convention. Its international audience is always hungry for new heroes to be celebrated by the design magazines, themselves often better looking than Vogue. The spontaneous buzz in this milieu is much more decisive than any kind of official promotion, and this was the kind of reception afforded to Droog. Designers, critics, curators, and writers were all drawn toward Droog Design with an unanimity which at first relied more on instinct than on rationality, but eventually was further confirmed by a deeper examination. When all the design buffs read the recurring statement in the opening of every non-Dutch text on the group, 'Droog' means 'dry' in Dutch, everything made sense. Droog kicked into place as the right thing at the right time.

'Dry' has a curious connotation: strong and clear like a good Martini, the desert, or a pointed remark in a conversation. Droog Design came at a moment when no one in the material world seemed able to tolerate redundancy anymore. Proof of this was and is everywhere, then in 1993 and still today. Droog's work ushered in the beginning of what some labeled the neo-minimalist era, a healthy and welcomed systemic revolution that has lowered our blood pressure and has transformed us into much cooler human beings.

In about 1993, when Droog was born, its brothers and sisters in the fashion world began to celebrate the work of Miuccia Prada and Tom Ford, the two who, with bareboned yet sophisticated simplicity took garments one step beyond the previous Japanese avant-garde. The exceptional Prada collection featured synthetic fabrics and clear A-cuts reminiscent of hospital nurses' uniforms. Very hygienic. Japan was the first country to market air by offering whiffs of pure canned oxygen for sale in street-vending machines. Elsewhere and the first in North America, the O2 Spa Bar in Toronto offers scented oxygen to be inhaled through cannules inserted in the nostrils. On the wave of the wide success of dispensing air as a commodity, branches of the bar are being planned for other cities on the continent, including New York.

More recently, in May 1997, at a symposium at the San Francisco Museum of Modern Art devoted to the theme 'Icons', art historian Alexander Nemerov spoke eloquently about a new American icon, not just a product: bottled non-carbonated water. He joined the choir to point out an apparent need for a cleaner, purer lifestyle.

All over the world, contemporary design reveals that advanced technology is no longer the elevated, glorified, complex icon which was literally represented during the high-tech stainless-steel 1980s, but rather it is appreciated for its ability to simplify our visual and material landscape. In other words, for how it can simplify our lives.

As in fashion now, furniture is lighter and less formally obtrusive. Objects are small, more personalized and carry easier interfaces. Interestingly, much of the identity of things is surrendered to surface treatments and to colors, which have made a cheerful return after the hiatus of many years filled by the black and chrome tyranny. This new phenomenon also is assisted by the progress of technology itself which allows for many more variations and degrees of freedom within the same manufacturing cycle - creating a much more interesting material world.

All the while, visual redundancy has been exiled to the four-dimensional world of the Internet, where a still-embryonic design language bubbles away, tending to abuse each frequent programming innovation.

Nevertheless, such a price to pay is low considering the Internet's contribution to material design and how it has helped spread the new philosophy and enabled discussions and exchanges of ideas previously inaccessible.

A second, somewhat consequential conclusion shows that very high technology can coexist in a peaceful synergy with very low technology. A cleaner lifestyle is the goal, and any means, even craftsmanship, to achieve this end is good. Besides, craftsmanship is no longer considered to be reactionary, and advanced materials, such as the aramid fibers of Marcel Wanders's 'Knotted Chair' and the fiberglass of Hella Jongerius's 'Knitted Lamp' can be customized and adapted by the designers themselves. But the tools to work them to the final shape might not yet exist. Some advanced materials actually demand manual intervention, while some low-tech materials, like glass milk bottles, that respond (at least in appearance) to ecological needs, merely demand a crafts approach because of their essential nature. Experimentation, be it high- or low-tech, requires a hands-on approach, and the flexibility and novelty of the materials and manufacturing methods available today has stimulated the exploration of numerous possibilities.

A third conclusion concerns the reason why things are made and the ways in which they are used. Design trends are often accurate reflections of social change, and the economy and sensibility which envelop the world after an age of excess are very strong forces indeed. Morality, sometimes even moralism, is a recognizable feature of many contemporary objects. In good recent design, ethics are as important as aesthetics.

All in all, contemporary design is frequently experimental in its use of materials and often inspired by genuine necessity. Even so, it sustains elements of surprise and deep intellectual beauty because it relies more on invention and reduction than on the elaboration of previous styles. While Droog Design has carried this model to the forefront, examples can be found everywhere. Jasper Morrison and Sebastian Bergne in England, Alberto Meda in Italy, and the Campana brothers in Brazil are just a few of them. Bergne went so far as to design round translucent soap. They all have used either rudimentary or sophisticated techniques to reduce their work to almost impalpable shapes, much like fashion designers used certain techniques to produce the transparent clothing that was the hit of the 1997 collections.

Ramakers and Bakker were able to recognize these structural trends, which have since spread worldwide, in a number of Dutch designers who were at the time working individually. They did not necessarily have much in common,

but shared a similar sensitivity. This particular sensitivity, stemming from the earliest times, is typically Dutch and thus exquisitely dry. Grouped together, the designers' discrete techniques and approaches make a seamless statement. These Droog Design protégés celebrate a brand of ingenuity and economy which has been transformed into a coherent minimalist aesthetic. Their objects' apparent modesty has made them emblematic of what political correctness in design should be. The collection is representative of the state of design, the closest phenomenon in the design world to the new less-is-more approach.

Droog objects are very dry indeed, so visually spare as to look impoverished - an illusion supported neither by the manufacturing values nor the retail prices. These products, at times made of recycled mass-produced objects, often look like an ode to industrial design, yet their composition is carefully handcrafted and produced in limited series. The presence of technology in the Droog collection is an ideal representation of its new versatile role in design and of all the possible combinations.

From high to low, we first find the category of Droog objects that employ advanced materials (high-tech matter) and manual treatment (low-tech approach) to achieve an expressionistic minimalism. Besides the already mentioned 'Knotted Chair' and 'Knitted Lamp' which belong to the subcollection called Dry Tech made in collaboration with the Aviation and Space Laboratory of Delft University of Technology, another good example is the recent 'Droog Design for Rosenthal' collection, presented at the 1997 Salone del Mobile. Gijs Bakker's take on the classic Rosenthal 'Accent' teapot features entwined ceramic fibers that replace the traditional solid ceramic handle. The fibers are glaze-melted onto the pot; the oldest and newest form of the same material - a ceramic - meet and the point of fusion is left dramatically evident. The high-tech objects in the Droog collection are often about this synthesis of past shapes and new techniques, or at other times about the synthesis of the image of old techniques, such as knitting or knotting, and their surprising realization in advanced materials.

Minimalism can also be found in other Droog products made with standard or mid tech processes, such as in Oval's inflatable lamps, Ed Annink's multipurpose hooks, and Arian Brekveld's 'Soft Lamps'. Most of these objects are oddly soft versions of normally hard objects. In particular, Hella Jongerius's approach to this idiom began with her polyurethane 'Soft Vases' of 1995, and it continued through 1997, the year we were introduced to entire washbasins made of the same material. Mid-technologies are substituted and thwarted to change the status quo and cunningly deceive our expectations.

Last, the exquisite low-tech approach, which echoes the poetry of the longer life cycles for everyday objects and is best represented by some of the first Droog milestones. In addition to Tejo Remy's talkative 'You Can't Lay Down Your Memories' chest of drawers and his 'Rag Chair', his 'Milkbottle Lamp' and Rody Graumans's '85 Lamps', together with Arnout Visser's 'Archimedes' letter scale and 'Salad Sunrise' oil and vinegar bottle, have become icons of the Droog collection. Public success comes as no surprise as the masses seem to favor Dada-esque compositions of found objects. Both an illusion of political correctness and an elementary sense of humor bring these objects closer to a world audience. While the Voorburg-based company DMD (Development, Manufacturing, Distribution) is Droog's favored manufacturer of primarily mid-tech products, many other objects are still either fabricated by the designers themselves or subcontracted to other manufacturers in the Netherlands. Recalling a model of production that can be found in the history of Italian design, Ramakers and Bakker work within a flexible network of small ateliers, traditional manufacturers, manufacturing plants, craftspeople, and high-tech transfer centers. With this stratagem, they maximize the resources appropriate to each item in the collection and maintain an open system joined or abandoned by individuals - all without harm to the collective.

It is not surprising to see that Dutch design is at the forefront of design today, not only cleansing the world but also blow-drying it. Droog's version of this contemporary less-is-more attitude has proved prophetic. Should it ever go mainstream, its legacy is already there: there is nothing cooler than dry.

Paola Antonelli, Associate Curator, Department of Design and Architecture, The Museum of Modern Art, New York

'We wanted to focus the problem of designing a bookcase on the bookcase itself, not proceed from a particular technique or material. First there are the things to go in it, books in other words. You can choose, then, between leather and paper. And because we wanted to make the bookcase as thin as possible, we chose paper. But also because it's basic and less pretentious.'

Rody Graumans, 85 lamps, 1993
70 r 100 cm, 15 watt lamps Manufacturer: DMD, Voorburg

'I'm not into that "less is more" stuff. I just work in lowly situations, like with an ordinary lightbulb, things that don't have much value. I like the idea of getting power out of inferiority. You can't avoid using a lightbulb, it's always part of a lamp's construction. And you shouldn't gloss over the bit you can't escape by sticking a shade over it.'

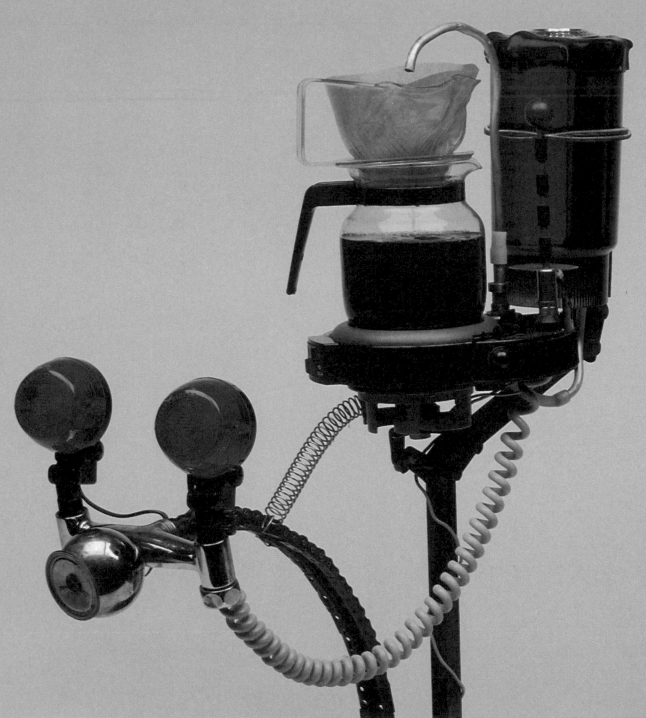

This coffee maker is assembled from reject material, including an old Braun hot plate, a piece of toothed belt and the base of an old transformer containing a sample so that the appliance really can 'speak'.

Hella Jongerius, Vase 'Urn', 1995
18 x 22/10 x 12 cm, soft polyurethane Manufacturer: Hella Jongerius

The shape of this vase is
familiar enough, so why think
up a new form when there
already is one suitable on
every count? The vase hides
nothing, the traces of its
making are still there. The
vase is a mass of scratches
and bubbles, the edge is
frayed, even the moulding
joins are visible. There is
nothing to tell us how old
this vase is. One more
scratch or stain would make
little difference to the way
it looks.

Arnout Visser, Salt glass, 1995
5 x 19 cm, glass Manufacturer: REEL, Rotterdam

The salt cellar works according to the principle of the hourglass. When the object is returned to the table after use, the salt runs back in a thin stream.

The table serves a double purpose, as a table but also as a plaything or a carrier of information.

Hugo Timmermans, Orangebox cupboard, 1993

100 x 46.5 x 210 cm, red cedar No longer in production

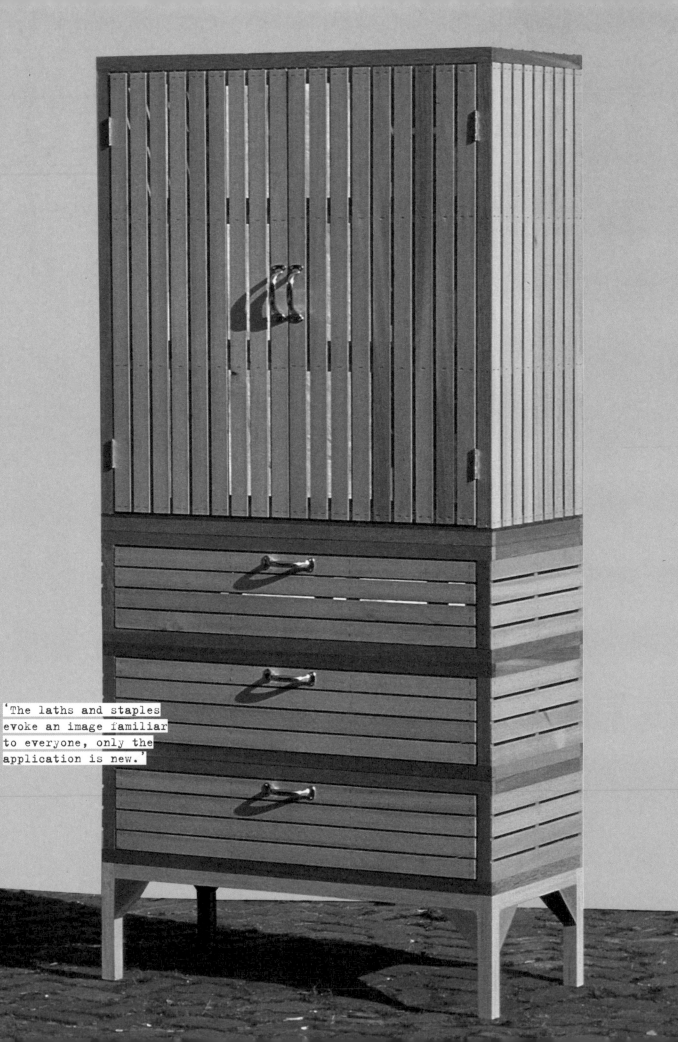

'The laths and staples evoke an image familiar to everyone, only the application is new.'

The starting-point is non-form turning into form through the qualities of the material. A basic shape is pushed inwards, which makes the top fall over. Differences in the thickness of the skin determine its final shape.

It all begins for Richard Hutten with the archetypal image of a table. His designs are premised on the 'Ur-table' consisting as this does of a table-top, four legs and supports: 'The table is not "given form" but "a given form".' By repeating, stacking and changing the dimensions of these basic elements, a new image emerges.

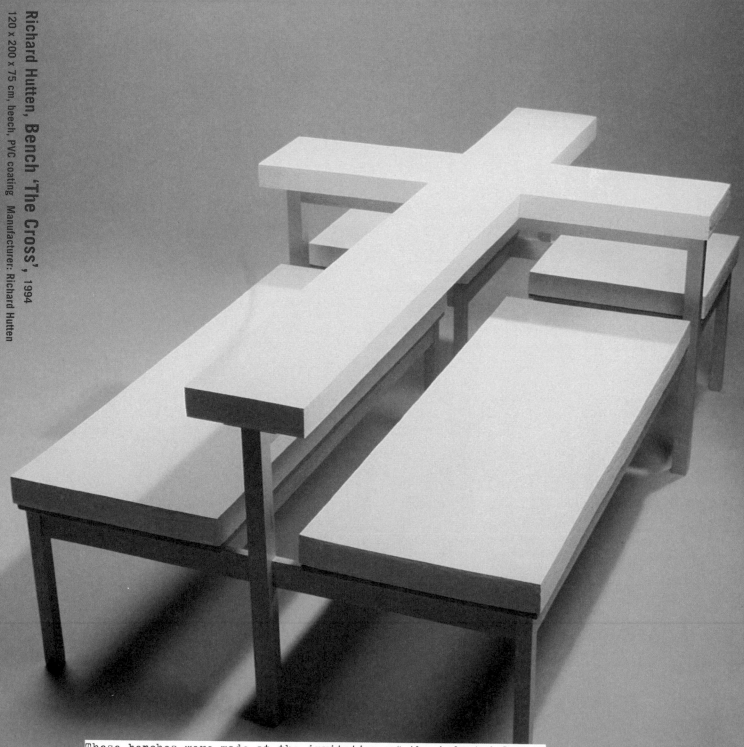

These benches were made at the invitation of the industrial fair 'Abitare il Tempo' in Verona as a part of the exhibition 'A Journey to Italy'. The designer took as his departure-point the political intrigues in Italy. The cross-shape, as Richard Hutten says, 'was inspired by Catholism in Italy, a breeding ground of corruption, fascism and misuse of power'.

Richard Hutten, Bench 'S(h)it-on-it',
110 x 110 x 75 cm, steel, varnished MDF Manufacturer: Richard Hutten

During the showing of these seats in Milan visitors scratched the words 'nie wieder' and 'never again' in the swastika bench. These inscriptions have become part of the design.

Spirit
Ninetie

of the
es

by Renny Ramakers

Spirit of the Nineties

Renny Ramakers

From design without limits to back to basics

'After years of fruitful experimenting we have reached a point where the New Design is no longer merely a sporadic expression of marginal groups.' With these words, Andrea Branzi and François Burckhardt set the scene for their exhibition 'European Capitals of New Design. Barcelona, Düsseldorf, Milan, Paris'.[1]
It is 1991. A new decade has just dawned. Ten years have passed since the Italian design group Memphis put on its first show in Milan. Ten years of particularly fruitful experimenting: an all-out confrontation with the rational and analytical design that had developed since Bauhaus days. The psychological, symbolic and poetic values of the product now came to the fore. Designers eagerly dipped into all available resources and didn't hesitate to mix them: high culture, low culture, no culture; home-grown and foreign; present and past, high-technology and crafts. The rules of good taste - the principles of unity, truth and logic - were sent flying on all sides.[2] Products were made by hand in limited editions. Intuition and fantasy ruled the day. Everything was possible, there seemed no limits to what one could do. In the eighties, design anarchy had overrun all Western Europe and beyond. Each country had its own version. If French designers toyed lightheartedly with elegant styles from their own past and with primitive cultures, in Germany, where Bauhaus tradition weighed heaviest, designers ransacked the contents of building marts and garden centres to strike an anti-pose often bearing an aggressive streak. The New Design was heterogeneous, a cauldron seething with individual expression. The developments in the New Design of the nineties as manifest in Droog Design, are inseparably linked with the design revolution of a decade earlier. One might even argue that Droog Design would not have existed without the pioneering work of Memphis, Alchimia and others. At the same time, we can identify a movement in the opposite direction. Memphis and Alchimia are typical phenomena of the eighties. The recipe that the New Design concocted in the nineties was altogether different, though many of the ingredients were the same. Droog Design too emanates the spirit of the eighties, at once perpetuating that spirit and at odds with it. But Droog Design is firmly welded to the Dutch mentality as well. Here we see a rift with Dutch tradition that is quintessentially Dutch.

For most European countries the rupture with 'old' design came quite suddenly. Not so in Italy. Memphis and Alchimia, the driving forces behind the New Design, were the end-product of fifteen years of experimenting on the fringe. Their source lay in the pop culture of the sixties. The initially critical and radical posture of those years continued to reverberate in Studio Alchimia, established in 1976, and would culminate in the eighties with the nihilism of its spokesman Alessandro Mendini. Alchimia was intended as an experimental laboratory in which all the visual disciplines fused. Furniture was used as clothing, old crafts were given the kiss of life, design classics were ironized. In 1980 Alchimia presented the project 'Banal Design' at the 'Forum Design' exhibition in Linz, Austria. Everyday objects, amongst which a mirror, a pair of shoes and a helmet, were systematically redesigned to a fixed scheme of colour and form. 'It was like designing objects that were immediately to emerge from hibernation,' as Mendini would describe it five years later. But his mood was anything but optimistic: 'This deliberately nihilistic approach, self wounding and cynical, allowed us to identify ourselves with the total blackout, to identify ourselves with the situation in which designers are unable to provide any answers.'[3]

Memphis by contrast, founded in 1981 with the support of industry, adopted an overtly anti-ideological stance from the word go. Barbara Radice points out in her monograph on the design group, that they were looking not for solutions but for possibilities. Their aim before anything else was to blaze new trails.[4]
Memphis did not counter the unbridled mania to consume, nor even denounce it. For Ettore Sottsass, founder and mainspring of the group, a liaison with the consumer society was inevitable. This was dictated by the zeitgeist, he felt: 'If a society plans obsolescence, the only possible enduring design is one that deals with that obsolescence, a design that comes to terms with it, maybe accelerating it, maybe confronting it, maybe ironizing it, maybe getting along with it. ... And then I don't understand why enduring design is better than disappearing design.'[5] Memphis did not criticize

the consumer society but denounced instead the modern movement which, caught up in its own principles, ignored the developments in society, the fact that western society had fragmented into a multiplicity of cultures, and paid no heed at all to the language, the symbolic value of the product. Memphis, rather than seeking ways of resolving the problems of society, sought instead to redefine the position of contemporary design. It immersed itself in all facets of contemporary life, being inspired by it to send out stimuli, high-powered stimuli. As Sottsass put it in an interview with the German theoretician Jochen Gros: 'Traditional modern design resorts to the most basic elements of product language. It says that the impression we should get of an object must come from the construction; that the most important thing we should be able to read in an object is its function; that colour must be so applied as to bring out the product's construction and function, and so on. We of Memphis say the opposite, we say O.K., this is all very important. But because we already consume so much imagery through photography, television, magazines, film and the like, and so fast, we need to produce stronger stimuli, more concentrated, more rapid, more complex.'[6]

The New Design of the eighties was keenly interested in semiotics, the theory of signs, as projected onto the consumer society by the French philosopher Jean Baudrillard.[7] In our post-modern consumer society with its continually increasing stream of products, Baudrillard postulates, the use and symbolic value of products is replaced by the sign-value; that is,

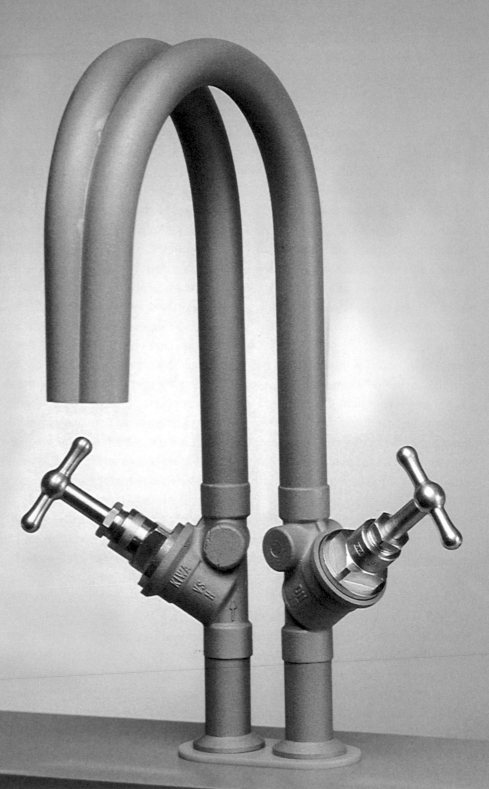

'My designs are rooted in my enthusiasm for forms born of purely technical requirements: industrial material, pipe assemblies, tools, building materials, and so on. The aesthetic quality of these products rests in their simplicity, the direct relationship between function and form. Their user-friendly, enlightening properties are in stark contrast to the affectations of design today. This prompted me to start searching for the "true" nature of a product.

products are increasingly construed as signs, as a code distinguishable from other codes. Sottsass and company were preoccupied with the meaning of objects in today's everydays surroundings, and with manipulating that meaning. This is Sottsass on laminated plastic: 'It's a material everyone detests. No-one wants to have it in the dining room or living room, it gets stuck away in the kitchen or bathroom. It's cheap, it's cold, it has nothing to do with status, has no tradition, has not the slightest effect on our feelings, it's godawful, and so on. We know that. But, what happens then? A piece of furniture entirely covered in laminated plastic is a durable form and looks transcendental into the bargain.'[8] The experiments of the eighties were geared to the consumer culture and capitalized on the almost limitless possibilities of the post-industrial era. The ebullient designs made at this time symbolize the society of excess, the 'throw-away' society, the era in which the sky was the limit. Studio Alchimia sent it up, the Germans waxed sarcastic about it and Memphis drank it in. Everyday culture in its many outward forms, from Hollywood kitsch to the tarmac of the Autobahn, had become a source of inspiration. There was no more moralizing about 'kitsch' and 'bad taste'. These had become an unavoidable part of reality and a potential source of great beauty.

The influence of these movements was manifold. Most important and fundamental is that the new spirit for many designers meant liberation from the straitjacket that the profession had become. The arsenal of means and sources of inspiration was expanded considerably, down to and including everyday culture; design dogmas were thrown overboard. For some this meant a freer outlook on design within the existing framework, for others a step towards a completely free practice rooted in a personal vision. Another important effect was that the gaily-coloured, uncomplicated designs brought the profession into the public eye. All at once design was fun. Functionalist design had been too distant to enjoy a greater popularity outside its own circles. Particularly Memphis, which has been characterized as the world's most popular avant-garde movement, caught on a big way.[9] Though Memphis designs have never been mass produced, their stylistic features were soon absorbed by popular culture. At the end of the eighties, the Italian group's influence was noticeable everywhere: in shops, on television, in cafés and restaurants. Unfortunately, it was the external characteristics in particular that were taken over, the dots and stripes, the gaiety and colour, with the result that 'design' began leading a life of its own as a style. Only the strongest are able to bear the luxury of unlimited freedom. A handful of designers managed to develop along renegade lines, such as Ron Arad who works like a sculptor.[10] The lion's share of designers, however, began wallowing in superficial fiddling about. The manifest character was gone, and caprice gained the upper hand. By the end of the eighties the movement had been sucked dry. It had become mannerism, form without substance. By then, Memphis itself had wisely disbanded.

In 1988-1989 the international arena showed the first signs of a change in mentality that would usher in the spirit of the nineties. The most radical was the installation 'New items for the home' which the English designer Jasper Morrison presented in Berlin in 1988. Of course there had been others before then within the New Design, such as Zeus in Italy and GINBAN<u>DE</u> in Germany, who had translated their ideas into simple, even minimal forms. But Morrison's installation has the character of a statement made at the right time. It was a glimpse into a spartanly furnished room with wooden floors and walls. In the bare space stood a couple of wooden chairs and a table. On the table were a number of objects for use, including three green bottles. The contours of a bookcase and a door were drawn on the wall, on which hung a

Jasper Morrison, 'New Items for the Home Part 1', 1988, installation for 'Designwerkstatt Berlin'.

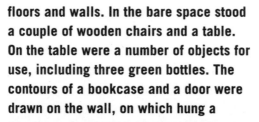

GINBAN<u>DE</u>, 'Tabula Rasa', 1987.

'Progetto Oggetto', 1992, a project by Jasper Morrison and James Irvine for Cappellini.

simple wooden coatrack. This room, which would have a sequel in Milan the following year, seemed to be calling the design world to order, to a back-to-basics approach. There is nothing neo-modern about this gesture, however. This is still the spirit of the New Design talking. Morrison is appropriating the same freedom. And shows the same keen interest in recycling elements from everyday use. But he commits himself to products of all ages rather than to today's consumer culture. Here archetypal forms are stressed, values that seemed destined to vanish. He does not trivialize, nor does he ironize, alienate or exaggerate. All that is accentuated is the beauty of the bottle, or the wooden coatrack with metal hooks still sometimes to be found in schools and old cafés, the beauty of the vernacular. These were redesigns, though you would scarcely notice; the essence had remained intact. In Morrison's case it is not the 'transience' of the consumer culture but 'durability', not visual stimuli but the obviousness of everyday artifacts. Morrison: 'It would be ridiculous if everyone always just kept looking for an attractive new form, it can be more interesting to look at what there is already, and to try to apply it in a different way.'[11] The coatrack and bottles were incorporated in 'Progetto Oggetto', a project he did with his fellow countryman James Irvine for the Italian furniture producer Cappellini and which was presented during the Milan furniture fair of 1992. It consisted of a collection of small objects, 'necessary and not so necessary' for everyday use in the home, many of which gave the impression of having been around for years. This idea of re-designing traditional objects for use was worked out in Progetto Oggetto by a number of young designers, such as the German Konstantin Grcic who added to the familiar wooden coathanger a clothes brush. It is striking how often minimalism was taken to the limit, almost to the point of being purism. Yet in many cases it is mainly a case of styling - there are no new inventions. But there are no frills added to create an ambience or distinguish an object from the rest either. In fact rather the reverse takes place: all frills have been removed. The product is stripped down to its essence. The Progetto Oggetto collection is clearly 'Some items for the home' taken a step further. The drawn contours of household goods on the wall in the Milan show, are a literal reference to the 1988 creation.

In many circles at the end of the eighties a desire for simplicity prevailed, for the familiar, the archetypal, the sustainable but also for 'establishing contact with those forms of design not yet tainted by western culture', as the young furniture manufacturer Giulio Cappellini described his motives for including a traditional Chinese seat in his collection.[12] There was undeniably a longing for purity, a search for the essence but also for traditional values, for memories. It is not the consumer culture that these designers tap but the very things that withdraw from that consumerism. Take 'Mobili di Servizio', the collection that the Italian firm of Lapis presented in Milan in 1988 in association with Bruno Munari, Alessandro Mendini, Aldo Cibic, Adolfo Natalini and others. It included small practicable wooden furniture pieces, of types that had almost become extinct in the design world: a set of librarian's steps, a wall shelf for books, a console, a plant-table. 'Silent attendants of domestic life', as Pier Carlo Bontempi, the project's artistic leader, described these products in the cata-

logue of the exhibition of the Lapis collection in Stuttgart: 'Indeed, these items of furniture don't impose, they communicate simply by being there. A position equal to that of rejecting the overwhelming surfeit of stimuli afflicting every imaginable design object these days.'[13] The items were presented in Milan as a counterweight to nihilism, the high-speed life and the state of perpetual change. They were an attempt to reinject a sense of morality into designing.

In these years we can likewise identify a longing for old-fashioned domesticity. In 1989, the Italian design critic Cristina Morozzi describes the trend as 'Neo-Liberty'. At that year's furniture fair, the high-profile companies had made the presentations homely before anything else.[14] Both Alessandro Mendini and Andrea Branzi had preached the uniting of miniaturizing information technology and domestic crafts. 'Post-industrial society and the electronic revolution will lead to more and more time being spent at home, time for working, studying and living. Domestic dwelling will become central to our lives,' as Branzi wrote in 1987.[15] In the years 1985 and 1986 he had worked on the 'Domestic Animals' project; a range of contemplative objects for 'a new domestic civilization'. Branzi described their style as 'Neoprimitive', particularly because of the use of arche-

Cappellini, exhibition in the showroom of Romeo Gigli, Milan, 1989.

Konstantin Grcic, Clothes-hanger-brush, produced by Progetto Oggetto from 1993-1997. Photo: Eva Jünger.

Pier Carlo Bontempi, Library steps, 'Lapis', 1988.

Andrea Branzi, Bench 'Domestic Animals', 1985.

Tejo Remy, Rag chair, 1991
60 x 60 x 110 cm, rags, wood frame, steel strips   Production: Tejo Remy

Tejo Remy's products are a critique of the glut of objects, the excess consumption in our society. Fact is, he wants to begin again, like a kind of Robinson Crusoe who keeps himself alive on his desert island with what he can find.

typal symbols and materials. In these hybrid objects modern technology (industrial materials) has been combined with wholly natural elements (tree trunks).

Towards the end of the eighties, the focus of attention shifted from outer to inner values. Not the addition of tantalizing stimuli nor a return to functional monotony, but rather a longing for products that were simply themselves. Design critic Ezio Manzini launched the concept of 'semiotic pollution' for the welter of images and signs, too many for us to consume. The paper he gave in 1989 at the ICSID congress in Nagoya, Japan, made a deep impression. He suggested that many of our current forms have no meaning. Products acquire meaning with the passing of time, through use. However, developments proceed so rapidly, he explained, that many objects for use have no chance to acquire real meaning. Products should really be granted a longer useful life.

It was in this period that the notion of recycling acquired new substance. At the beginnings of the eighties, young radical German designers in their abhorrence of the design establishment, had turned with relish to the ready-made. A shopping trolley became an easy chair, a sieve a fruit bowl. These strategies stood in stark contrast with the recycling design of the German Des-in group of the seventies, who had acted out of serious environmental commitment, their most audacious design being a couch assembled from used car tyres.

In the eighties this awareness of environmental issues slipped somewhat into the background, but as the decade ended it returned as a subject of wider interest. An all-encompassing environmental policy emerged in numerous countries. In the Netherlands, for example, the first 'National Environmental Policy Plan' appeared in 1989. Industry was coerced into taking environment-friendly measures and research into this area started on all fronts, including experimenting in design. In 1989 students at the Hochschule der Künste in Berlin for instance did a project for General Electric Plastics that focused primarily on the recycling of products and materials. In the nineties, environmentally-conscious design figures prominently on the agenda of industrial designers. Recycling simply has to be done.

Some designers saw the environment and its attendant issues of disposability and planned obsolescence, as a new source of inspiration. In 1988 the Russian-American designer Constantin Boym presented his 'Recycle' collection at Gallery 91 in New York. In that same year Kunstflug, a design group based in Düsseldorf, which since its inception in 1982 had warned of the environmental repercussions of large-scale industrial production, presented 'Projektion der Stile', a wardrobe assembled from cardboard boxes.

Des-in, Car tyre couch, 1975.

Axel Kufus, Fruit bowl, 1984, for 'Kaufhaus des Ostens'.

Constantin Boym, 'Recycle', 1988.

Kunstflug, Hardy Fischer, 'Projection of styles', 1987.

dd-22

Tejo Remy, Chest of drawers 'You can't lay down your memories', 1991
110 x 120 cm (variable), various types of used drawers, maplewood Manufacturer: Droog Design

'Each drawer carries its own memories and these are all jumbled up in your head. So the chest must be just as chaotic.
The great thing about it is that it trains your memory. You have to remember exactly what went into which drawer.'

Moulded in one piece, the razor folds open at the handle when the blade needs changing. The 'hinges' are integrated in the material. The shaving brush consists of a bunch of bristles held together by a flat ring and a hoseclip. The product shows what a shaving brush is essentially – a bunch of bristles.

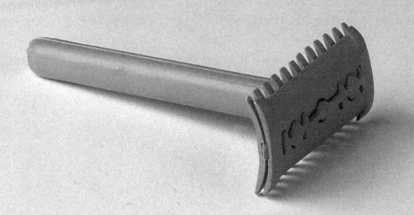

The aesthetic qualities were made apparent by the slide projected onto it. As Hardy Fischer of Kunstflug put it: 'It's about solutions in the course of a design process, which might lead to the disappearance of objects altogether. The idea that each distinct function has to have a machine or tool of its own, is tantamount to a crime in ecological terms. We think it's enough to exchange software.' [16]

In the Netherlands, Tejo Remy in particular was concerned with the recycling element. His graduation work of 1991 included a 'chest' of used drawers, a rag chair and a milk bottle lamp.

The developments in the Netherlands, as these would come together in Droog Design, carried the spirit of the late eighties into the nineties, needless to say in the worthy company of designers from elsewhere. As the nineties began so did the Gulf War, throwing the world into a brief economic crisis. Now 'the new sobriety' was not only informed by a longing for stillness and the environmental issue; economic necessity had become a new contributory factor.

Simple forms and simple materials prevailed in modern furniture design of the early years of that decade. Sobering down had become a social phenomenon. The concept of sustainability, both physical and aesthetic, was all at once a major issue.

In the meantime, though, we continued to wallow in excess. Each year brought endless new variations on what already exists - a chair leg bent a little further here, a chair rest articulated slightly there, a tartan design for a chair seat which had been plain the year before.

Even the new sobriety produced little more than variations on a new theme. The beginning of the nineties saw a galaxy of simple, mostly wooden furniture designs pour from the drawing board with 'back to basics' as the guiding principle. Libération, the French daily, would be prompted by the Milan furniture fair of 1993 to write that 'only a few contributors have shown that stillness is synonymous with tranquillity rather than with boredom.' [17]

Companies in the forefront of experiments in the eighties became realistic in the new decade. In the press release on its presentation at the Milan furniture fair of 1992, the German furniture company Vitra announced its wish to show that the experimental energy of the eighties had now gelled in new products. Now was the time for consolidation. Many designers who had followed their own imagination a decade earlier, now committed themselves to industry or education. The New Design as it evolved in the eighties, has become an accepted phenomenon but it has lost much of its verve in the process.

Sobriety and recalcitrance

'Less is more'. With these words, Dutch designer Benno Premsela ended his contribution to the catalogue of the exhibition 'Made in Holland' on show in the Museum für Angewandte Kunst in Cologne in 1995. Mies van der Rohe's dictum gave Premsela a cut-and-dried definition of Dutch identity. And the products showing at Cologne confirmed it. Whether designed in the thirties, forties, fifties, sixties, seventies, eighties or nineties, they were invariably subdued, clear-cut and rectilinear of form. [18]

On observing this unbroken production of abstract geometric shapes, a comparison with the rural landscape of the Netherlands suggests itself: no mountains or impenetrable forests but a man-made composition of polders with straight lines and simple forms. Not a single detail has been overlooked. This is not that surprising, however, in a landscape largely wrested from the water and kept in balance by a system of hydraulic engineering. Besides, with upward of fifteen million inhabitants on a surface area of scarcely 42,000 km^2, careful planning is an absolute necessity. The Dutch live in the most artificial of landscapes, where nothing has been left to chance. The tendency (and the need) to subjugate, manipulate and structure nature is an inseparable part of Dutch culture: so the relationship with nature is by and large functional.

This country's affiliation with the artificial and its population's inner compulsion to regulate everything is, as it were, sublimated in the work and ideas of Piet Mondrian. According to Mondrian technological development should culminate in the complete suppression of nature and so open the doors to absolute beauty. Stripping down his paintings to compositions of lines and planes, primary colours and non colours, he set out to express the finely tuned proportions of the artificial era to come.

Mondrian's striving for clarity, aesthetic order, reduction and purity is anything but an isolated phenomenon in the Netherlands. Abstract geometry runs like a leitmotif through Dutch design.

But we might also identify a link with the mercantile spirit and with Calvinism. Formerly, the Dutch saw themselves as a nation of 'traders and preachers'. The traders being the mercantile upper-middle class, or the city burghers consisting as they did of patricians and 'regents'. This was a free-thinking layer of the population which adhered to a moderate, obliging, liberal Protestantism informed by the teachings of Erasmus. The preachers by contrast represented the strict, orthodox Calvinism which found most favour among farmers, fishermen and the lower-middle class. Here, religious constraint was uppermost. [19]

Frans Hals, 'Regents of the St.Elisabeth Hospital, 1641'. Collection Frans Halsmuseum Haarlem.

Both groups shared a sober-minded streak. Seventeenth century portraits of well-to-do merchants and regents are literally a picture of restraint and frugality. The clothing is black, the 'frills' stop at broad white collars and cuffs. The Dutch generally are not given to ostentation. The pomp and circumstance that overtook palaces and churches elsewhere hardly touched their country. Symbols of power and status mean little to the Netherlands.

This does much to explain the reaction in the eighties to Memphis and Studio Alchimia. Thus in 1984 we find the Dutch art historian Hein van Haaren sounding the alarm against 'indolent Milanese design... a dangerous fashion that shirks critical self-analysis.' And continuing his sermon, he condemned the elitist character of the objects, not only for their artistic pretensions but because they were incomprehensible to 'the masses'. [20]

Hugo Timmermans, Coated Canvas Cupboard, 1993

150 x 120 x 40 cm, beechwood, canvas Manufacturer: Hugo Timmermans

The canvas acts as a stabilizing surface-filling element within a minimal timber structure.

'Act normally, that's quite crazy enough' is a popular saying in the Netherlands. This is the clear-headed, practical business instinct speaking, an instinct that is often recalcitrant enough to regard 'acting crazy' as quite normal. A true paradox of Dutch culture.

Resistance, dissent if you like, is a national habit. The Dutch have centuries of civil protest to look back on, in fact this nation's history begins on such a note. Love of freedom, recalcitrance, intractability and anti-authoritarianism are qualities that the Dutchman holds dear. Campaigning is in his blood. Even conservative groups and those representing authority will clamber onto the barricades should something incite their wrath. This is a game the Dutch people and the authorities play together. 'It's a paradox: unconventional behaviour is conventional in the Netherlands', as Ernest Zahn postulates in his study of Dutch society.[21] Such behaviour is tolerated, so long as it doesn't affect the rights and freedom of others, according to Zahn; thus the entire country could witness on television how the Minister of Education appeared dressed as Santa Claus offering university fees to demonstrating students.

Dutch government is all for an unconventional image. The police cruise about in white Porsches with vivid stripes that recall the world of advertising rather than authority. Recently police officers in Amsterdam have even taken to roller skates. Dutch bank notes, rather than depicting heroic figures, show simple everyday subjects - a snipe, a lighthouse, a sunflower. For the all-important marks of authenticity, the designer of these notes was given the green light to smuggle in all manner of personal passing fancies, such as his signature and fingerprint, even his pet rabbit.

'Holland ist Dada', joked the German artist Kurt Schwitters in 1923 in his magazine Merz. Together with Theo van Doesburg, the driving force behind De Stijl, he baited the public at Dada soirées. And it worked. Whether out of approval or opposition, the public responded wildly. It blared, crowed, shrieked, whistled and argued away.[22] Similarly averse to convention, of course, was Gerrit Rietveld's celebrated Red-Blue Chair of 1918 and his equally famous Schröder House of six years later. Also in his later work there are idiosyncratic moments aplenty: take the Zigzag chairs and furniture made from packing-crate wood of the thirties, or the easy chair of 1942, folded out of one piece of aluminium.

R.D.E. Oxenaar and J.J. Kruyt, Bank note for 250 guilders (lighthouse).

Studio Dumbar, Corporate identity for Dutch police force, 1994.

The sixties in the Netherlands as in other Western countries, were brimming over with nonconformist phenomena. Campaigns, happenings and Fluxus festivals grew into a veritable cult. Since then the nose-thumbing element has been a thoroughly ingrained part of Dutch art and design. In 1991 the Rheinisches Landesmuseum in Bonn presented 'Schräg/Tegendraads', an exhibition featuring 'parody, humour and ridicule in Dutch art, photography, film, fashion and design'.[23]

In Dutch graphic design both the geo-

Marion Herbst, Case with bracelet and salad
basket, 1975, perspex and aluminium.

Gijs Bakker, Penis-cube, 1970,
elastic textile knitted in the round.
Photo: Ton Baadenhuysen.

Gijs Bakker, Stovepipe necklace, 1967,
anodized aluminium.
Photo: George Herwaarde.

metric abstract tradition and the non-conformist strand came into full flower. The strict functionalism of Wim Crouwel and the poetic purism of Walter Nikkels populate the graphic landscape in concert with Anton Beeke's provocative theatre posters, Studio Dumbar's downplaying graphic approach, the former experimental magazine Hard Werken and the politico-radical aspirations of Wild Plakken.

Of great importance for later developments in Dutch product design is the revolt of the jewellery designers in the sixties. They wanted to shake off the atmosphere that had always surrounded jewellery. Theirs was a protest against a commodity valued by the materials it was made of, diamonds and gold, rather than by its design; an aversion to a product that had investment value and served as a status symbol. The key representatives of this movement were Gijs Bakker and his wife Emmy van Leersum. In 1967 Bakker, in an audacious move, presented a necklace and bracelet made from stovepipe. The couple designed large metal collars and headbands that emphasized the relationship between jewellery and clothing, between jewellery and body. Clothing and jewellery converged in experimental garments, such as the tightfitting tricot suits of 1970 in which protruding

and jointed parts of the body were stressed by solidified plastic shapes such as a penis-cube or a breast-case.

Many personal ornaments designed by Van Leersum, Bakker and others like them, ground-breaking though they were, fitted neatly designwise into the Dutch design tradition that had been evolving since De Stijl: minimal shapes in smooth industrial materials. Repercussions were soon to follow. In the early eighties, Marion Herbst began her own revolt against this 'slick Dutch' style, setting up in 1973 the League of Rebellious Metalsmiths. She was calling for a looser, freer, more downplaying modus operandi.

In the seventies, jewellery design turned increasingly to cheap everyday materials and ready-mades. In 1975 Herbst designed a case containing a metal salad basket and a bracelet made from such a basket. Three years later Maria Hees created a range of bracelets made from lengths of garden hosepipe, and a brooch made by sticking the bristles of a round hairbrush through a pullover.

Many jewellery designers at that time were hooked on the ideal of low-cost series production and some ended up in product design as a result. Industry however was not interested at all. These designers were too idiosyncratic and their designs too modern. Those who wanted to continue saw no other way than to produce and market their products themselves. Bruno Ninaber van Eyben and the duo Frans van Nieuwenborg and Martijn Wegman were among the first of those trained as jewellery designers to produce their own wares. There was no choice, though by no means all designers regarded this as a disaster. Some were eager to take care of production themselves so as to control the process right through from idea to end-product. Generally, batches were limited yet successful products did emerge, such as Bruno Ninaber van Eyben's pendant watch which has made its way all over the world.

During the course of the seventies, the number of designer-entrepreneurs was to expand rapidly. A major influence on this tendency was Gijs Bakker, who lectured at the Arnhem Academy of Visual Arts during the years 1970-1978. He taught designers to act independently of industry, not to wait for commissions but rather concentrate on their own development. He urged his students to see themselves as free artists, and like free artists to build up an oeuvre of their own. 'I was rallying against the sweat-of-one's-brow image of the industrial designer. All design motifs at that time were based on functional requirements. Industrial design was cloaked in a pervasive seriousness as if it were a hellishly difficult job. For me it was something like "we can do that too",' recalls Bakker. Such maverick behaviour caused irritation in the industrial design world, which spoke condescendingly of these 'goldsmiths parading as industrial designers'. Reactions like these only stimulated the renegade designer-entrepreneurs who began to produce a stream of lamps, vases, clocks and fruit dishes. Their approach was, however, severely formal in the finest Dutch design tradition. The objects are smooth and rectilinear, usually having no other meaning than a balan-

ced relationship between function and form. The conceptual approach of the jewellery designers or their use of readymades made little headway in product design, even in cases where designers were working in both disciplines. Apparently, the designing of furniture and other objects for use was considered to be industrial design and thus had to have an industrial look. Since De Stijl and Bauhaus, the abstract-geometric form had been regarded as best suited to industrial production, and the seventies were no different. We would have to wait until the following decade for this to change.

The Netherlands is absent from the exhibition catalogue mentioned at the beginning of this essay, 'European Capitals of New Design'. Yet in the eighties numerous Dutch designers had been inspired by the New Design. At a show of Dutch furniture at the Bouwcentrum in Rotterdam in 1983, Ed Annink's chair stood out like a sore thumb. The seat is set obliquely on the metal frame and covered with artificial grass. One year earlier, Annink had designed a lectern in the shape of a butterfly to visualize the effect of speaking in public. In 1985, the Centraal Museum in Utrecht invited him to design a postmodern period room. His arrangement combined pieces designed by like-minded colleagues with antique furniture.

Bruno Ninaber van Eyben, Pendant watch, 1976, black anodized aluminium, rubber neckcord, Swiss quartz.

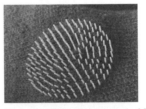

Maria Hees, Hair-brush brooch, 1978.

Frans van Nieuwenborg/Martijn Wegman, Neck-zip, 1973. Photo: Anna Beeke.

Ed Annink, Lectern, 1982, fibreboard, artificial grass, metal, plywood, plastic.

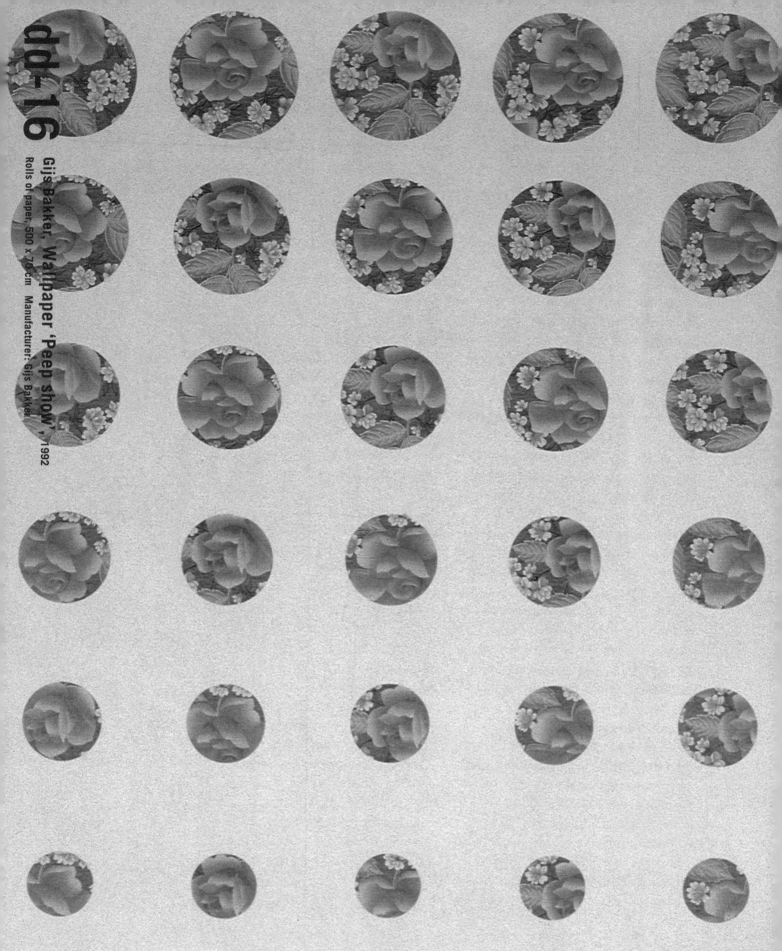

Gijs Bakker, Wallpaper 'Peep show', 1992
Rolls of paper, 500 x 70 cm
Manufacturer: Gijs Bakker

The look is determined less by the wallpaper itself than by the wall underneath, retaining a link with the past.

This chair was originally
designed for the project
'Chair Sweet Chairs',
initiated in 1989 by the
Products of Imagination
foundation, The Hague.
Bakker was one of fifteen
designers invited to give
a basic chair structure its
definitive shape.
Bakker: 'I wanted to made it
lighter, both visually and
physically. So I drilled some
holes in it. The greater the
demands made on the construction,
the smaller I made the holes.
The chair lost almost a third of
its weight that way.'

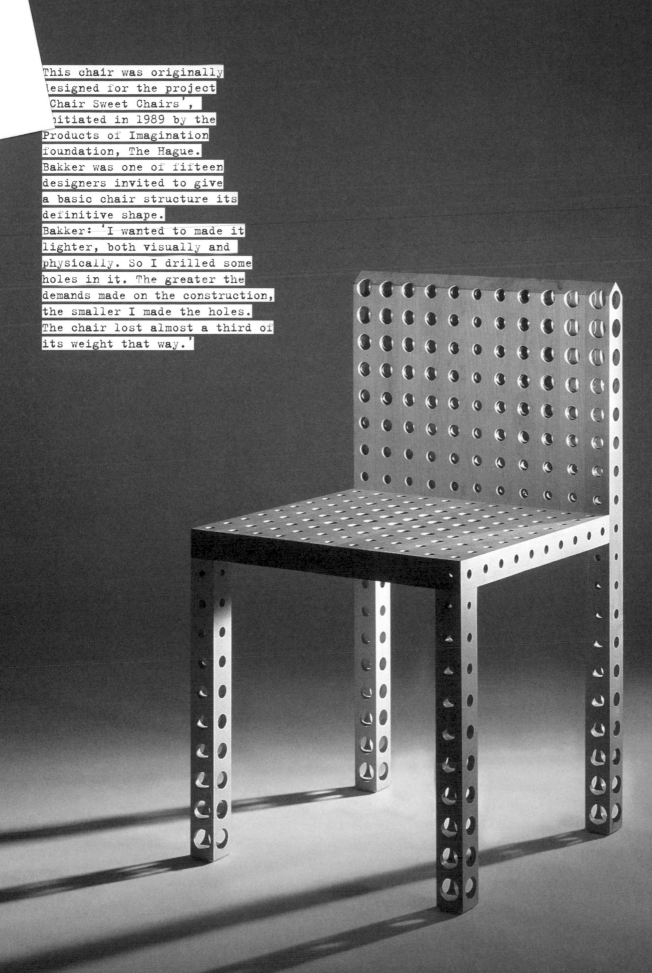

Central to the new Dutch design was the wish to bestow meaning on products. The hegemony of abstract geometry, form for form's sake, needed to be broken down. These designers didn't bother with means of production or functionality. Where the 'artist' aspirations of the previous generation seriously concentrated on series production of realistic products, to this new wave of designers the inner driving force was all that mattered. However, the New Design as it evolved in the eighties in the Netherlands, never really managed to take root. By and large two trends can be observed: first an investigating, largely theoretical approach, marked by ideas that often seem forced, more sketches than objects for actual use. In 1984 Jaap van Heest designed a series of nine small cupboards that all looked precisely the same when closed yet each opened in a different way. As to how each cupboard opened and what was in it was left to the users and their memory. In exploring the relation between people and objects, Van Heest had taken the side of the latter, that is to say, had embraced the 'insurrection of things'. This trend further manifested itself in closely argued attempts to break down archetypes. Ed Annink focused on designing a chest 'with no identity' and 'no functional relationship with furniture archetypes'. Jaap van Heest endeavoured to shift the table top away from its usual place.

Of a similarly exploratory nature if less theoretically premised was the work done at this time by Peer de Bruyn. With a deep sensitivity for materials, he concen-

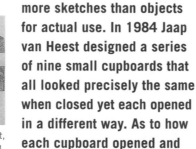

Jaap van Heest,
Nine small cupboards, 1984.

trated on the associative and intrinsic value of materials which had hitherto been merely imitative or inferior by their very nature. In 1983, armed with a series of self-produced cupboards, he engaged in polemical discourse with the Dutch oak furniture manufacturers who were and still are in the habit of advertising their wares as 'solid oak', 'semi-oak', 'oak veneer' or 'imitation oak' without there being any visible difference between them. Later De Bruyn tried to upgrade the 'inferior' materials of hardboard and chipboard.

The second trend marking the New Design in the Netherlands was an emotional, associative tendency heavily influenced by Bořek Šípek. This Czech designer who had been based in Amsterdam since 1983, had an exhibition of his work in the museum Het Kruithuis in 's-Hertogenbosch in 1986. Šípek worked in an organic style that stressed the personal and the associative. So too did the efforts of his epigons. Their products carry loaded titles, have ritual functions and are executed in exclusive materials. But the Dutch designers failed to reach the Czech's high spiritual and substantial level. Whereas Šípek's work, as personal as it was, quite clearly referred to the nature of the objects, many of the Dutch designs got no further than an autonomy that today seems forced. The designs themselves were often affected and introverted. There was no link, moreover, with the country's culture. The Dutch New Design of this period gave no clear new direction. The products were loaded with meaning but were largely subdued and aesthetic in appearance. Designers tried desperately to inject their work with personal associations or to fundamentally change its intrinsic qualities.

The semiotic charge of Memphis and Alchymia made only a superficial impression in this country. Dutch pragmatism prevailed in the end. Modernism was too deeply rooted here. Most attempts to shake off Modernism along all manner of associative detours, clung closely to the Dutch tradition of clarity, restraint and straightforwardness or deviated in too contrived a way. The developments in Dutch design in the eighties can best be characterized as attempts to return substance to the product, to do away with rectilinear abstraction, the legacy of De Stijl, and throw fossilized principles overboard. But, however free designers felt, moral duty weighed heavily. Designers continually felt obliged to justify themselves, to weigh up good against bad. Take the following text written in 1987 by Wilma Sommers, representing the emotional, associative tendency, whose laborious soul-searching is a far cry from the self-evidence with which, say, Mendini elaborates this theme: 'In what relation does decoration stand to design, when is it permitted (who decides this?) and when isn't it? Is it only added flavouring and if so, what's wrong with that? Should decoration be functional or is decoration a function from the start? Should the decoration be considered per object, if it's fitting, and for whom? Or is all decoration inappropriate because it's about decorating? Is colour a decoration? A curved line? Or is it in fact the strict straight line which is the decoration? Is decoration always a lie because of its concealing nature or because man can only take a small amount of truth?'[24] The Dutch Calvinist heritage is apparently not to be escaped that easily.

At that time, the game played in the design world with decoration and associations was still in full swing. But it was not to last for much longer. In 1988 Marcel Wanders fashioned five basic lampshades into a new table lamp. His motive was not to explode archetypes as in Jaap van Heest's case, but to recycle them. In this he can be compared with Jasper Morrison, though the means Wanders employs are even more subdued, and their application a good deal more extreme. He does not minimalize the traditional lamp. All he uses is the shades (in fact the most archetypical element), yet stacking five of these creates a new image that breaks free of the lamp archetype. The restraint of the means is contradicted, or compensated, by the way they are applied. This paradox is even more strongly present in the chandelier Rody Graumans designed in 1993. Once again, the components could not be more elementary: a lamp bulb, a wire and the necessary connectors. But there are no less than eighty-five of these in combination, upgrading the simple bulb into an opulent chandelier. This is 'less is more' in its most literal form - perhaps 'more of less' would be a better description.

The new sobriety that arrived on the international design scene as the eighties ended, is in perfect keeping with the abstract simplicity of the Dutch design

Peer de Bruyn, Cupboard, 1986, hardboard, oak, chipboard, filler, 110 x 100 x 45 cm. Collection / Photo Centraal Museum Utrecht.

dd-35a/b

Eibert Draisma, Moving lamp 'Sinus' / Moving lamp 'Cosinus', 1990

Manufacturer (made to order): Eibert Draisma

50

The two hinged lamps are assembled from existing components; each moves in its own way, resulting in an exhilarating dialogue.

51

tradition. But a new generation has emerged that interprets this proverbial Dutch tendency towards basics in quite another way. Bidding farewell to the style of De Stijl, these designers set out to produce style-less products. This new generation absorbs the everyday culture very literally. Ideas are still at the centre, but no longer introverted or narrative. They refer instead to contemporary product and design culture, and reject the polished style of established design.

Piet Hein Eek, Scrap-wood cupboard, 1991.

Products are back to just being products, not references to all manner of attendant issues. And ideas are translated into concrete, usable objects. Still no serial production or functionality as the basic premise, just the concept, though serial production has indeed proved to be a possible end result. Here, the Dutch tradition of simplicity and clarity links arms with the nose-thumbing element.

The new and the familiar in close harmony

It is no longer surprising to find in, say, an article on the water and energy consumption of tea kettles the category 'design kettle'. The word Design has become epithetic. 'Design design' has seeped everywhere. The vacuum cleaners in the average electrical supplies shop look alike yet they are all slightly different. Each one has been 'designed', meaning that a designer or stylist has been to work on it and given its technology a look just that fraction different from that of other vacuum cleaners. In our multiform society the ideal of a uniform mass production no longer works, yet one might wonder just how differentiated the current production really is. The profession has fallen into the vice-like grip of the market.

And the cycle continues. What began in the eighties as deep-rooted criticism of a bloodless functionalism went on to suffer the same fate. Form, however meaningful it was originally intended to be, has become form without meaning. Designers are urged to keep inventing new forms, a demand that is increasingly difficult to satisfy as more and more variations descend on the market. This can only lead to so much bric-à-brac.

Things are presented as 'Design objects' and as such acknowledged, assessed and condemned outright: 'It looks beautiful but it doesn't work'. Design is expected to be smooth and stylish, with all irregularities ironed out of it. Quality is synonymous with perfection.

As the nineties dawned, the Netherlands was hit by a flood of reactions to the design profession's emphasis on beautiful materials, careful detailing and a perfect finish, on design with a capital D.

In 1991 Piet Hein Eek graduated at Eindhoven Academy of Industrial Design with a cupboard made of 'the most evil scrap-wood' he could find. The cupboard was built up of floorboards from houses due for demolition, old timber with the paint peeling off. Eek wanted to show that even ugly materials and a rough-and-ready finish could produce beautiful

'Some things just look the way they look and basically that's all right with me. What interests me is taking a thing that everybody knows and doing just enough to it to make it that bit different.'

products. His cupboard had splits and cracks all over it, but this didn't seem to matter. It is part of the aesthetic of the object. In fact the colours produced by the paint flaking on the wood only enhance the qualities of the cupboard, giving each piece its own identity. Eibert Draisma, while studying at the same academy, designed between 1989 and 1991 a series of coffee makers assembled from discarded merchandise, oven dishes, preserving jars, bicycle lamps and the like. Not only the exterior of these objects is unconventional, the whole idea of coffee-making is approached from a unusual angle. One appliance, exploiting the changes in pressure, transforms during the coffee-making process into a thermos flask, another literally tells you when the coffee's ready, accompanied by flashing red lights. His graduation project unleashed a storm of discussion among the academy teaching staff as to just how much this coffee maker could be classified as industrial design. Hadn't all the elements been borrowed from another context? And what exactly was the designer's input? That he had looked through forty-odd oven dishes before finding one of suitable dimensions, just as another designer might have drawn as many profiles on paper, evidently failed to convince the august body.[25] The upshot was that Draisma was allowed to graduate 'officially' on a 'designed' version of one of his coffee-making creations.

The comparison thrusts itself upon us with the way the industrial design establishment had responded ten years earlier to Gijs Bakker's coffee maker which was every bit as maverick as Draisma's. When making it Bakker had ignored the standard aspects of production and marketing. His only concern was to visualize the process of making coffee. In his case, though, everything had been 'properly' designed. It was the amount of visible metal components that got his design blacklisted. Such appliances ought to be designed in plastic for injection moulding, was the 'official' opinion.[26] Tejo Remy was another young designer to step distinctly out of line. Graduating like Draisma in 1991 but this time at the Academy of the Arts in Utrecht, Remy made it quite clear that he didn't wish to design. He wanted to start again, so to speak, making things from what he could find - like Robinson Crusoe, as he put it. This was not only a swipe at the drifting state of established design but also at the glut of objects, at the excessive consumerism afflicting our society.

His chest of drawers was particularly radical. Improvisation is the name of this game. Remy collected twenty old drawers from here, there and everywhere, knocked together a wooden frame for each, stacked them any old how and strapped the lot together with a belt. And that was that. This was Remy protesting against the sheer complexity of the design profession. And of course the established order was not always amused. 'This isn't design', the 'official' industrial design world cried. That the chest has no fixed form is also a bone of contention. You can strap it together as you wish, swap drawers around or, as one owner did, include a TV set among them. But when the Droog Design exhibition was held at the end of 1995 in the Kunsthal in Rotterdam, staff of the Boijmans Van

Beuningen Museum (lender of the chest) were most careful to see that it was assembled to exactly match the arrangement in the picture!

In the first half of the nineties, the accent in this type of design lay on the assembling of existing products or components, used or otherwise. That this design mentality is generally associated with environmental issues is understandable. This certainly held true for some designers but for them it was more a way of thinking than keeping strictly to the letter: in no way did it mean applying the rules of environment-friendly design. In fact many of the designs were in direct contradiction of these rules. Tejo Remy in packing each used drawer of his 'chest' in a new container of solid maplewood wasted more than twenty recycled drawers could compensate for. In Remy's case environmental issues figure strictly in the background. As he himself says, 'I am not offering a constructive solution, I'm not solving anything'. The environmentally thoughtful side of the work of those designers resonates in the distance it takes from the short-winded stimuli of the contemporary product culture and from the pressure on the designer to keep creating something 'new'. There was clearly a search on for a design appropriate to the spirit of today, for another aesthetic experience.
In the mid nineties, when the accomblage boom passed its peak, these premises would remain. Even when young designers turned to plastics, by then rehabilitated as ecologically sound. In 1995, Hella Jongerius designed a vase of soft polyurethane. Instead of inventing a

new form to suit the material in hand, she unceremoniously ditched the 'to each material its own form' principle and used a classic shape with its roots firmly in ceramics. Why invent a new form when there already is one suitable in every respect?
If the shape of this vase is familiar enough, the combination of form and material is not, most especially the way the material has been treated. The vase hides nothing, the traces of its making are still there. We can clearly see how the polyurethane has been scraped out of the mould; the vase is full of scratches, the edge is frayed, even the moulding joins are visible. There is nothing to tell us how old this vase is. One more scratch or stain would make little difference to the way it looks.
Hella Jongerius's vase touches on the question of visual durability, which in the case of plastic is very short-lived indeed. Plastic products age visibly but don't develop a patina. They are expected to look smooth and shiny on the display shelf. How they look after a period of intensive use, seems to matter less. All products are by definition designed to look new. But the smooth perfection of today cannot permit the slightest scratch. It is one of the reasons why things get thrown away.

'What's your favourite product - your real favourite? Ten to one it's not that flashy bit of high-tech you've just bought, but something old, something a bit worn, that's been with you a long time, something with which you go back a long way.' This comes from the 1997 issue of Philips Design, which goes on to announce

These floor tiles are made of polyurethane mixed with glitters. The hologram structures give the floor an illusion of depth. The image changes with the incidence of light and the viewer's position.

that 'ageing with dignity' is a key target for the Philips design team.

This graceful ageing of products looks like becoming the design ideal of the nineties. In our 'throw-away' society with its incessant call for innovation and its apparent inability to resolve environmental issues, we seem to be yearning for 'eternal beauty'. Hella Jongerius chose a classic shape for her vase. The architectural firm of MVRDV decided to spread Persian carpets on the floors of the building they designed to house the VPRO radio and television company in Hilversum. 'Non-design gives you room to move', as MVRDV put it.[27] The Dutch architect Willem Jan Neutelings is fond of the word 'laziness' in this context. In his opinion, there is nothing that says that a designer has to do something; it is often better to leave things be. 'In our day, there's this misconception that you always have to be doing something. The entire social culture is geared to it.' 'Every year', Neutelings continues, 'there are new corkscrews invented just because the leaves start sprouting on the trees. It shows a lack of restraint, with form and colour as major issues and not a moment given over to reflection, to a thought process where restraint takes over. You often arrive at better or at least different results by doing less. The danger is, I feel, that the whole profession - and this can be as much design as architecture and planning - is tuned to originality. Originality as the ultimate goal. Whereas my opinion is that recycling old ideas in a good way, using them again without copying them has a far greater quality.'[28] Not everything needs designing anew. At times it is better to leave things as they are. Apply this to the letter, and designers would be left with little to design, particularly those specializing in furniture and home accessories. The dilemma of a respect for tradition, the desire for enduring products, against the yearning for things new, will never be resolved. People love to have new things, companies will need to continue innovating, times will keep on changing.

There has long been a belief in the enduring nature of the modernist model, in the timelessness of simple, minimal forms. The firm of Braun showed this to advantage in the German presentation at the 18th Milan Triennale held in 1992 and wholly devoted to 'the challenge of the environment'. Braun's accompanying text referred to 'long-lasting design made for ten, twenty, even thirty years' and the ecological value of timeless design, simple, minimal. But this has failed to hold water for years now. Modernist minimalism has proved to be a period product after all. And, as we have seen, there is the utterly damage-prone, smooth perfection of this type of design.

In 1995 Stuart Walker, writing in Design Issues, proposed a combination of macro-simplicity and micro-complexity: visual simplicity in the overall design and visual complexity in the surface treatment. The latter he describes as follows: 'The qualities which a micro-complex surface could exhibit include texture and variation in texture, variation in color, irregularities in contours, diversity in finishes from glossy to matte, and intentional "imperfections".'[29] Hella Jongerius's polyurethane vase designed that same year illustrates this theory perfectly. Intuition can shore up theory, even anticipate it.

Richard Hutten, Bench 'Split Level', 1995
120 x 60 x 70 cm, beechwood, PVC coating. Manufacture: Richard Hutten

Lowering part of the table-top produces a sitting area and a backrest. The 'table-top' looks hard but turns out to be soft to the touch and comfortable too.

Sustainability may also coincide with transience. A product should be able to visibly tarnish without necessarily becoming more beautiful as a result. It just gets older, as we all do. You use a product until the thing falls apart. The time this process takes can vary. This is not that important in itself, so long as the product ends up in a cycle. This is far preferable above the brief lives led by fashionable trends. The Belgian fashion designer Martin Margiela, who has always been intrigued by weathered materials, demonstrated the beauty and naturalness of the ephemeral in the exhibition Museum Boijmans Van Beuningen devoted to his work in the summer of 1997. Margiela deliberately cultivated the mould clothes get when damp for too long. He collaborated with Wageningen Agricultural University on analysing exactly which colour effects could be achieved. The catalogue accompanying the exhibition even gives recipes to this end: mould as a pigment.

'Simply wearing out is no longer enough, it seems,' according to Dutch designer Marcel Wanders, 'things should either not wear out or look beautiful doing it; lack of respect for age is what it is, really.'[30] He proposes adding 'age metaphors' to products, something he himself demonstrates with his knotted chair, which applies the ancient macramé technique to high-tech fibres.
The macramé fabric gives the chair not so much an old look as a familiar one. You recognize it, but then again you don't. It is as though the chair has been around for years without you ever having seen it before.

Familiar things are important in our lives. But we do want new things too. A logical solution would be to combine the two - the familiar applied in a novel way. Products in the Droog Design collection that satisfy this condition include Tejo Remy's milk bottle lamp, Hugo Timmermans's orangebox chest assembled from laths and staples, Visser, Kwakkel and Van der Jagt's function tiles made from the standard white bathroom variety, and Konings & Bey's Kokon chairs, which envelop familiar chair shapes in an elastic synthetic material. Sometimes it concerns the use of brand-new everyday elements. At others, as evinced by Tejo Remy's chest of drawers and rag chair, used commodities are actually worked into the design. It may be the archetypal form that brings recognition, or it may be the traditional technique. Products become more familiar still when the user is able to inject something of himself into them, modify them in a personal way.
'You take away the human touch if things are not allowed to change', according to the Belgian fashion designer Ann Demeulemeester.[31] In the work table she designed for the Belgian firm of Bulo in 1996, its users are invited to leave their traces on it. The table top is covered over with painter's canvas on which the user can write, doodle and generally make a mess. When it gets too dirty, you simply paint over it. By this means, the user adds a personal touch to the design. The same holds for Gijs Bakker's perforated wallpaper which is meant to combine

Tejo Remy, Chest of drawers 'You can't lay down your memories', 1991. Variant with TV set, private collection. Photo: Eric Schilt.

with the old wall covering underneath into a pattern. Tejo Remy's rag chair can also work that way, as what would be more beautiful than to compile it from clothes discarded by its user? This way products can become part of the user's personality.

In fact everything revolves round the relationship between people and products. In the seventies things not only had to be functional, they had to look functional too. The eighties brought attempts to strengthen this relationship by designing 'totems', objects that evoke meaning. In the nineties the accent shifted to recognition, to the familiar. Everyday products, objects we all know but take for granted, are given a new look. High style has made way for low style, and even 'ugliness' gets in on the act. Some products go so far as to involve interaction: the user is invited to play an active role in the design, to set his own stamp upon it. The experiential aspect, placed centre stage in the eighties, is an important element in the Droog collection too. But with Droog it proceeds in another direction. Not because products send out a wealth of visual stimuli but by way of a subcutaneous level that proves to pleasantly excite the spectator. It is the paradox of recognition and surprise that excites the senses. Some call this humour, yet I believe that none of the designers seriously mean it as such. It is the concept - no more and no less - in which irony, an element of professional self-mockery, may of course figure. Some products reveal their true nature immediately; in others, this needs to be discovered. A vase proves soft when touched. The

exact purpose of the two glasses on a metal plate only becomes clear when you press the button. And sometimes you need to know the story behind a product to get at its deeper meaning. Why has the curtain got a dressmaker's pattern printed on it? Why flower-bulb packaging made of cow-dung? The answer lies in the product itself. The concepts are realized in the most straightforward way. In fact they are one with the product. Everything is left in view, nothing has been added or removed. Ultimately, these products are utterly revealing and insightful. Each is exactly what it represents, even if you are only aware of it on closer inspection.

Giving insight into the nature of the product is another way of strengthening the bond between people and products. Developments in electronics have put many products beyond their users' comprehension. Anything resembling a user-product relationship has then to do with optimum functioning or a compelling exterior. The innards are strictly taboo. The London-based designer Daniel Weil responded to this in the eighties by dismantling the black box of transistor radios and clocks and decoratively arranging the various parts in a see-through plastic bag. Similar aspirations inform Peter van der Jagt's doorbell. Not only is it quite clear where the ding-dong sound is coming from, the necessary technology normally hidden somewhere behind the button at the door is likewise brought into view where it contributes to the look of the thing.
Van der Jagt's doorbell along with other designs in the Droog collection occasionally ruffle the feathers of established

designers because of their lack of 'style', such as screws being left in full view rather than carefully smoothed away. But it is just these elements that make a product comprehensible and accessible, and who knows, easier to repair, an almost unheard-of luxury these days. If the glass on the doorbell breaks, simply glue on a new wine glass.

Such designs are not proffered as the ultimate solution to a problem or as the only direction to be taken, but more as opening the way to many possibilities.

Developments are proceeding at full tilt. A look back over only five years of Droog Design is enough to convince us of that. As we have seen, the accent in the beginning lay on assembling existing products and using simple materials like wood, craft paper and rags; designers turned to synthetic materials in the mid-nineties. The picture is perpetually changing. This might mean that old themes reappear, but then in a new guise. The polyurethane washbasin designed by Hella Jongerius in 1997 is the outcome of a quest in search of nothing other than the 'natural form' of this material. She achieved her aim by taking a 'non-form' and turning it into form through the qualities of the material. Decoration is back on the agenda too. Dick van Hoff, who graduated at Arnhem Academy of Visual Arts in 1996 designed a washbasin out of pieces of felt stitched together by a sewing machine. The zigzag stitches are a decorative element, though a decoration deriving from the process of making, one that increases the product's comprehensibility. In the plates Van Hoff made for the 'Droog Design for Rosenthal' project, decoration is the underlying concept. The designer distances himself from the customary technique of sticking transfers onto finished products and allows the decoration to stem entirely from the production process. He made a series of plates in which no two are the same by mixing clay and colour in the extrusion machine and letting the machine dictate the change of colour.

Every epoch, then, brings its own new ideas, its own drives, its own criteria. Piet Hein Eek's 'scrap-wood' cupboard of 1991 showed that imperfection can generate beautiful things. 'Droog Design for Rosenthal', the project presented six years later, demonstrates the opposite, namely that technical perfection can result in an unpolished appearance. In short, the important thing is not the nature of the design principles, as these change over time, but the current value of the idea behind a design.

But how does this fit into the mechanism of supply and demand?
These days it is the market calculations that decide which products get made. Designers have developed into full-fledged client-oriented enterprises. Design is regarded by a sizeable chunk of the profession as 'business'.
The design practices have gone professional and taken up a position as service companies working in concert with the clients. This attitude has thrown open wide the doors to industry but it has tended also to iron out the rough spots. There is little trace left of fundamental innovation, let alone intrinsic design quality. Middle-of-the-road reigns supreme. Economically, things are going well

Richard Hutten, Stool, 1994
50 x 50 x 40 cm, beechwood, PVC coating Manufacturer: Richard Hutten

That the sitting area is soft is only apparent when you apply a certain pressure (by sitting on it), which is why this product can double as a side table.

with design but in terms of substance the profession is in crisis.

Designers following their own vision are having a hard time logging into industry, if we exclude a handful of 'enlightened' firms. As a result many of these independent designers are producing and distributing their designs themselves. There are countless design labels circulating in the Netherlands alone. Modest design enterprises can on occasion burgeon into a full-scale company. Examples in this country include Designum, founded in 1980, and DMD, set up in 1993. The latter firm, which was set up with the intention of commercializing products designed from an independent perspective, has brought a whole host of Droog products onto the market.

The association between Droog and DMD has brought many designs into the real world. One of the first was Tejo Remy's milk bottle lamp, which DMD elevated to a full-fledged industrial product, an item that sells steadily in the shops. In the current flexible methods of production, craft and industrial production techniques, one-offs, limited batches and mass products are beginning to intertwine. The same should hold for independent and client-oriented designs. Hella Jongerius's polyurethane vase, which she makes individually in her studio on demand, now has a derivative among DMD's product supply. This version is produced in series and consequently has a more industrial look than the unpolished craft version, yet it upholds a degree of imperfection in that the air bubbles in the material are exploited as an esthetic element rather than regarded as manufacturing defects. Market-targeted design is for most companies an economic necessity but it can lead to an impoverishment of the product culture if there is not an independent vision to counterbalance it. Conversely, an independent vision can easily lead to a blinkered do-it-yourself attitude or an over-the-top autonomy, should it fail to find some outlet in serious industrial application. It's a question of striking the right balance.

Products like the ones featured in this book are regularly shrugged off as 'art'. Unjustly, I feel. Fortunately there are designers who do act independently as artists. This does not, however, automatically make their work autonomous art. The individualistic position charted within these pages sits fairly and squarely within the tradition and context of product design. And this is where it belongs, even though only one of any given product ever gets sold. It is of inestimable importance for the practice of design that things stay this way, that independent design doesn't become alienated from the design context. For one thing is certain - the design profession could clearly do with a good shake-up every once in a while.

Notes

1   Andrea Branzi and François Burckhardt (eds.) Neues europäisches Design, Berlin 1991, p. 6.
2   Such as formulated by Gustav Pazaurek, Guter und schlechter Geschmack im Kunstgewerbe, Stuttgart 1912.
3   Kazuko Sato, Alchimia, Never-Ending Italian Design, Japan 1985, p. 268.
4   Barbara Radice, Memphis. Ricerche, esperienze, risultati, falimenti e successi del Nuovo Design, Milan 1984.
5   Richard Horn, Memphis. Objects, furniture and patterns, New York 1986, p. 22.
6   Der fall 'Memphis' oder die Neo-Moderne, Offenbach Lectures, 25 and 26 January 1984. Hochschule für Gestaltung Offenbach am Main, Studies and materials, vol. 7, 1984, p. 37.

'The felt parts are sewn together with black stitching. The drainpipe is in grey PVC stitched into the felt. Then the whole gets impregnated with polyester resin. The design has to do with my criticism of the clogged-up attitude the sanitary industry has. A washbasin to me is a receptacle for catching excess water, no more and no less.'

7 Jean Baudrillard, La société de consommation,
  Paris 1970.

8 Renny Ramakers, 'Stoelpoten hoeven niet per se recht te
  zijn', interview with Ettore Sottsass in de Volkskrant,
  28 June 1985.

9 Richard Horn, op. cit., note 5.

10 See also Volker Albus and Volker Fischer, 13 nach
   Memphis. Design zwischen Askese und Sinnlichkeit,
   Munich, New York and Museum für Kunsthandwerk,
   Frankfurt am Main, 1995.

11 Renny Ramakers, interview with Jasper Morrison, in
   Preview. Design for Cor Unum Ceramics,
   's-Hertogenbosch 1993, p. 33.

12 Maarten Kusters, 'Alles mag en kan. Internationale
   Meubelbeurs 1988', industrieel ontwerpen 5,
   October 1988, pp. 26-30.

13 Hans Höger, Dienende Möbel, Strenges Glück. Kompakte
   Figuren, Stuttgart 1990, p. 23.

14 Cristina Morozzi,'Huiselijke burgerlijkheid', industrieel
   ontwerpen 6, December 1989, pp. 22-26.

15 Andrea Branzi, Domestic Animals. The Neoprimitive Style,
   Milan 1987.

16 Dieter Willich, 'Duits design onder de zure regen',
   industrieel ontwerpen 2, February/March 1992.

17 Brigitte Oller, 'Les sept clés du pret-a-meubler',
   Libération 30 April, 1 and 2 May 1993, pp. 41 and 42.

18 Gabriele Lueg (ed.), Made in Holland. Design aus den
   Niederlanden, Tübingen/Berlin and Museum für
   Angewandte Kunst, Cologne 1994.

19 Ernest Zahn, 'Regenten, rebellen, reformatoren', in Een
   visie op Nederland en de Nederlanders,
   Amsterdam 1991.

20 'Hein van Haaren over Neo-design', Items 12, 1984.

21 Zahn, op. cit., note 19, p. 27.

22 K. Schippers, Holland Dada, Amsterdam 1974.

23 Schräg/Tegendraads. Parodie, humor en spot in de
   hedendaagse Nederlandse kunst, The Hague 1991.

24 Products of Imagination. The Dutch Experiment in Design,
   Rotterdam 1987.

25 Anke de Jong, 'Eigenzinnige aanpak. Eibert Draisma stelt
   design met een hoofdletter D aan de kaak', industrieel
   ontwerpen 2, March 1993, pp. 36-40.

26 Renny Ramakers, 'One-off items and mass production', in
   Gert Staal and Hester Wolters (eds.), Holland in Vorm.
   Dutch Design 1945-1987, The Hague 1987.

27 Ida van Zijl, 'Het gevoel voor een stoel', Items 3, 1997,
   pp. 28-35.

28 Herman Moscoviter, 'Architect Willem Jan Neutelings; ik
   ben geen advocaat van lollige architectuur', Items 1,
   1997, pp. 36-43.

29 Stuart Walker, 'The Environment, Product Aesthetics and
   Surface', Design Issues, vol. 11. no. 3, 1995. pp. 15-27.

30 Eternally Yours newsletter 4, May 1996.

31 Liesbeth Mollert, 'Onbeschilderd doek op poten', Items 1,
   1997, pp. 44-45.

dmd-50

Arnout Visser, letter scale 'Archimedes', 1990

5 x 20 cm, pyrex glass   Manufacturer: DMD, Voorburg

The letter scale is based on the principle of Archimedes. The level in the water-filled-cylinder rises with the weight of the letter.

100

50

20

grs

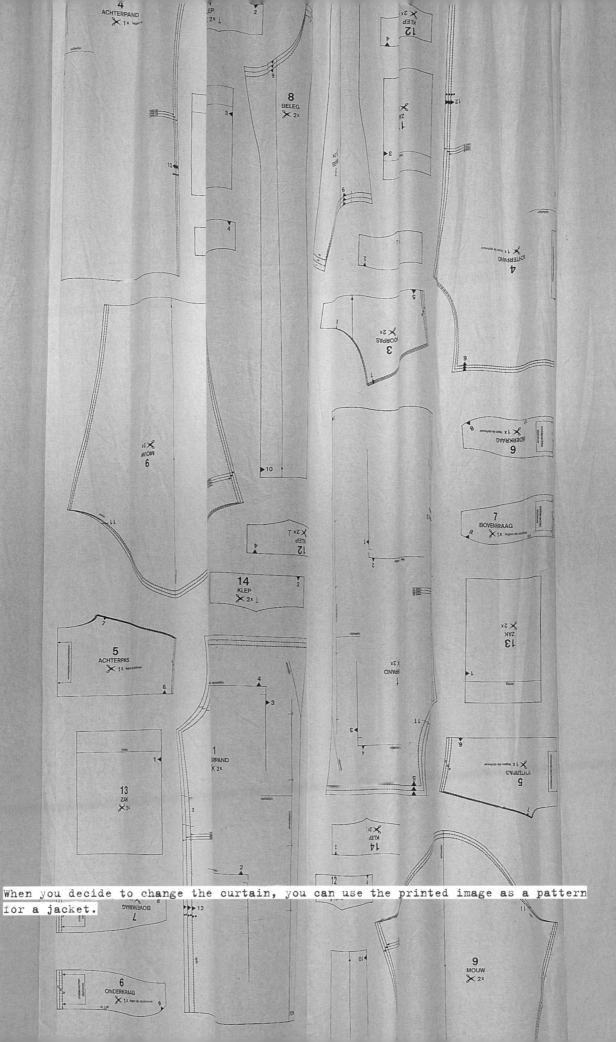

When you decide to change the curtain, you can use the printed image as a pattern for a jacket.

Martijn Fransen, **Easy chair**, 1994
75 x 55 x 70 cm, polyether, PVC coating, standard chair seat Manufacturer: Martijn Fransen

The standard seat is wedged into a U-shaped block of foam plastic. The flexibility of the polyether makes for more comfortable sitting and obviates the need for construction.

With this lamp the old PVC dip technique has acquired a new use.
Arian Brekveld: 'I tried to give the lamp the most subdued form I could.
I like the way the cord almost melts into the shade.'

Frank Tjepkema has tackled a very unusual theme: artificial plants. The traditional arrangement has been replaced by a pile of identical leaves on a rubber foundation. By using the existing ingredients in a different way, artificial plants are given an original quality.

dmd-89

Hella Jongerius, Soft vase, 1995

15 x 27 cm, soft polyurethane. Manufacturer: DMD, Voorburg

70

The air bubbles in the material are not regarded as unavoidable flaws but exploited as an esthetic element. Hella Jongerius: 'Polyurethane is mostly used as a material for making moulds, which was what prompted me to start the "rubber copies" project – restating existing forms in a new material.'

Arnout Visser, Oil and vinegar bottle 'Salad Sunrise', 1990

4 x 18 cm, pyrex glass   Manufacturer: DMD, Voorburg

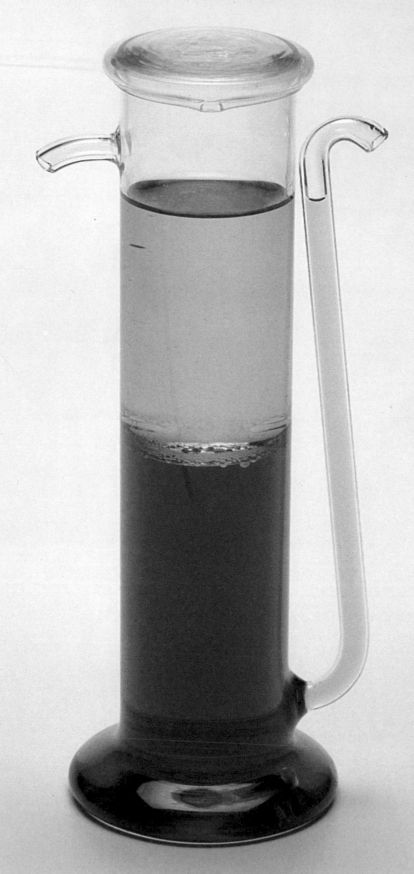

'I enjoyed doing things with different liquids; oil floats on water and that gives a nice effect. So I made an oil and vinegar set.'

Hella Jongerius, Bathroom mat, 1993
60 x 40 x 4 cm, soft polyurethane Manufacturer: DMD, Voorburg

Solidified drops of water to massage the feet.

Arnout Visser, Glass tap, 1997
25 x 40 x 30 cm, glass Prototype

The temperature of the water is made visible
by coloured light. If the water is hot,
it's red. Cold water has a blue colour.

Paul Hessels, Power tiles, 1995
15 x 15 cm, ceramic Prototype

Power point and tile in one.

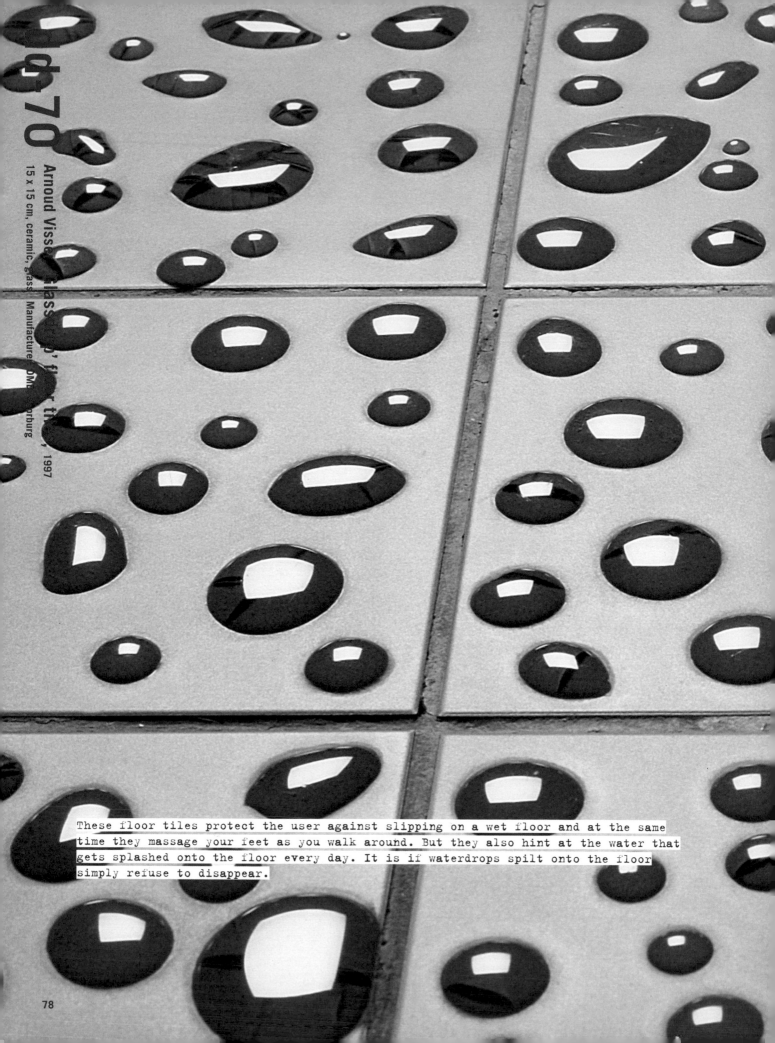

d.70
Arnoud Visser 'glassdrop' floor tiles, 1997
15 x 15 cm, ceramic, glass. Manufacturer DMP, Voorburg

These floor tiles protect the user against slipping on a wet floor and at the same time they massage your feet as you walk around. But they also hint at the water that gets splashed onto the floor every day. It is if waterdrops spilt onto the floor simply refuse to disappear.

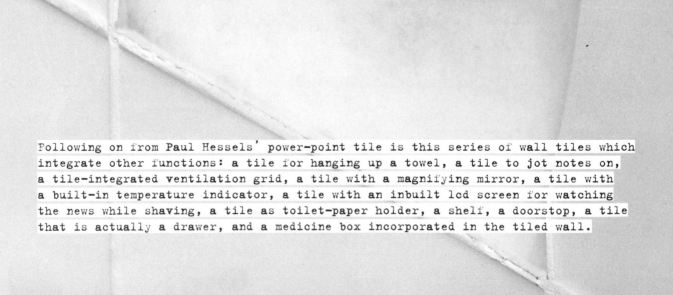

Following on from Paul Hessels' power-point tile is this series of wall tiles which integrate other functions: a tile for hanging up a towel, a tile to jot notes on, a tile-integrated ventilation grid, a tile with a magnifying mirror, a tile with a built-in temperature indicator, a tile with an inbuilt lcd screen for watching the news while shaving, a tile as toilet-paper holder, a shelf, a doorstop, a tile that is actually a drawer, and a medicine box incorporated in the tiled wall.

UHF VHF TUNING

OFF

Eating
Potatoo
a Silve

es with
r Fork

by Yvonne Brentjens

Eating Potatoes with a Silver Fork

Yvonne Brentjens

'High above Europe, flying from Padua to Amsterdam, I am reminded each summer that there is such a thing as a northern mentality. The chaotic pattern of the snowless Italian Dolomites. Germany; blotchy but neatly arranged. And then the Netherlands, an altogether ordered, structured, artificial world. And I am touched'.

'Een middag gewoon doen'
show in rock club Paradiso, Amsterdam, February 1993.

Back on terra firma Gijs Bakker remains the watchful observer; clear and articulate like his designs. 'There is no country in the world where design is as wide-ranging as in the Netherlands. Provincial towns like Purmerend or Flushing; wherever you are you may find a Driade bench, a Danese dish or perhaps even the Droog Design oil and vinegar bottle. Whenever I'm in well-to-do Italian circles, it's always a suffocating, traditional, history-bound environment; old houses crammed full of hand-me-down furniture. Antique, antique and more antique. In the very best instances, architects are prepared on occasion to add a lamp by Castiglioni or an armchair by B & B to their dust-laden possessions. What a contrast with the Netherlands where the tendency is very much towards contemporary things. And what a painful contrast with the frustrating situation for young Dutch designers, who in the Dutch society of merchants and salesmen have a hard time making headway.'[1]

Bakker's travel impressions outline briefly the conditions from which Droog Design emerged. Love and hate resound in his words; mixed feelings of hilarity and a deepseated loathing that he shares with the art historian Renny Ramakers. Both their accounts resonate with the image of the pragmatic Netherlander, descended from sellers of spices, who likes to see his warehouses well stocked. The physical restrictions imposed on him by his own small country, have made him methodical by disposition; a virtuosic builder of bridges, a travelling salesman who has always known what there is to buy in the world.

On window ledges, mantelpieces and drawing room tables, he shows off his beloved 'designer pieces'. International fashion, it must be said, excites his urge to buy, more than his own country's harvest wrested from the cold ground. Rietveld's red-blue chair, the national symbol of hardship if ever there was one, has never made us sink to our knees in humility. Van Gogh's The Potato Eaters has never inspired us to embark on a spiritual diet. And as for the holy words of Mies van der Rohe that express our rapacity so well, we would have preferred to have made them up ourselves: 'Less is more'. More, more, more...

And yet the calvinist in us has difficulty living with such a display of form. The unremitting flow of design products is ever pricking his conscience. 'Deep within us', wrote a Dutch critic not so long ago, 'there resides a hankering for the absolute form, as much concrete as abstract. A form that represents both the type and the individual example; a form-giving of proper nouns fixed in place by the definite article. Not a chair, but the chair, not a lamp, but the lamp...'[2] That fundamental longing will doubtless always be with us. But the utopia of the absolute form, as the only true outcome of unimaginative problem-solving, was abruptly dashed at the start of the nineties. 'Nowhere in the world', observes Ramakers, 'was the sudden resistance to Design as extreme as it was in the Netherlands.' With statements such as 'Who do we designers think we are? Gods making fine things for mortals?' and 'I don't design, as it happens; I don't want to design', a young generation singlehandedly exploded the myth of The Designer. In the prevailing lacklustre tug-of-war between less and more, between restrained and outgoing, between function and fiction, dogmas and dreams made way for people. The chairs, lamps and cupboards of this new generation - naked, unpolished metaphors - showed us what we were. Herd member or heretic, monk or monarch, disinclined to exertion, or simply disinclined.

It looked as if Bakker's sixties credo had been reborn. To use his own words, the form became the packaging for the idea. 'The round soft cuddly-toy design was pushed aside by forms that all at once brought the contents into view. Cultural, political or social, design became a means of communicating.' The designer hid his vulnerable thoughts no longer. Rather he got under the skin of the user, who like him had to live with his con-

science, with greed and hunger, with his head and his heart. No longer was the world's chaos streamline wrapped. The idea of progress shifted to one side. Designers shrugged at those starry-eyed idealists who sat fingers drumming in the post-paradise, waiting for the shock of things new.[3]

'Droog Design', exhibition at Pastoe, Via Cerva Milan, April 1993.

But what they got came more as a shock of recognition. Young Dutch designers seemed no longer interested in originality. They arranged, they assembled. Or, as Umberto Eco would say: 'Innovation is to be found in the way the material is ordered. Creativity is less a question of inventing than of reorganizing what is already there.'[4] Once the vain ruler over time and space, the designer had knowingly upended his own pedestal. Rodin's Thinker seemed to have been brought to life. The classic pedestal had become an ordinary chair.

Jan Konings and Jurgen Bey's paper book-case; Gijs Bakker's perforated wallpaper; Arnout Visser's oil and vinegar bottle - the sensation these and other designs created could have produced enough copy at the time. But Renny Ramakers, then editor-in-chief of the magazine Industriëel Ontwerpen, decided to try another tack. She opted for bodily confrontation, visual design criticism as she calls it, dubbing the event 'Een middag gewoon doen', an untranslatable name that meant that this was to be a private viewing with no frills, no Sunday best and

Andreas Möller, Flower bulb packaging 'Bolle-Box', 1994
8 x 8 x 8 cm, compressed dried cow dung Prototype

preferably no high-flown conversation. In other words just acting normally, which is quite crazy enough, as they say in Holland.

The memory of that wintry Sunday afternoon of 28 February 1993 is not without its romantic side. As if only the murky past had a patent on those informal, hastily improvised meetings in establishments later recorded in block capitals in the literature. Take the café Hotel de Notre Dame where Karel Appel and cohorts chopped logic. Or the Dadaist debauchery in Cabaret Voltaire. A similar uniquely excitable atmosphere was destined to reign in the Amsterdam rock club Paradiso. Everyone was there, as though they had sensed in advance that something special was afoot. True, Piet Hein Eek's 'scrap-wood' cupboard was loaded in again in the evening. But that didn't matter, now that it had been in the middle of things. Everyone took the sensation home. Wrapped in newspaper along with an oil and vinegar bottle or milkbottle lamp. That afternoon in Paradiso, without anyone realizing it at the time, a new chapter was added to Dutch history. All things considered, it was a last-ditch attempt. A final move to confront the media and profession in this country with what at that time could well have been the most 'ordinary' designs anywhere. So ordinary that the extremeness of their simplicity and restraint threatened to go unnoticed. So ordinary that they were simultaneously too wacky for words. Snow may have covered the polders and fields, but Dutch grass hadn't looked that green for ages.

It was on that day that Droog Design was born. Not the name, not the foundation, not the very first collection - but the largely accidental synergy of two minds: Renny Ramakers and Gijs Bakker. Two outsiders in a hermetically sealed world of insiders who realized that it was high time to confront that world with the new world of everyday. Like two salesmen carrying just the one case. That afternoon they decided to join forces and lump their ideas together. Now that the pedestal had gone, the design temples had lost their lustre. Without further ado, curatorship was unceremoniously removed from its smug museum context and the cultural body of ideas plonked down elsewhere; at an event where exhibitionism has reigned supreme since the year dot - the Salone del Mobile in Milan.

'Droog Design', exhibition in the Kunsthal, Rotterdam, December 1995/January 1996. Exhibition design: Konings & Bey with Roelof Mulder. Photo: Ernst Moritz.

There are enough earlier examples of such patronage as that hastily improvised by Ramakers and Bakker. But an exact historical equivalent is more difficult to find. The early twentieth-century motivator Karl Ernst Osthaus can be excluded as being too inclined to group into styles. Again, those avid collectors the Kröller-Müllers were far too possessive. And while Napoleon III who founded the Salon des Refusés comes reasonably close, his ventures ultimately proved too politically tinged. Perhaps the artistic maternal role that publicist Bertha Zuckerkandl played in early twentieth-century Vienna, fits Ramakers the most

'Droog Design' exhibition in INTERNOS-DONNA ELISSA, Via Bernardino Luini, April 1994. Exhibition design: Ed Annink.

snugly, as Oskar Schlemmer's well-worn coat sits best on the designer and teacher Gijs Bakker. Yet they themselves would never endorse the terms spiritual father or mother. Quite the reverse in fact. In April 1993, the Dutch designs making their first journey to Milan, remained the brainchildren of product designers who were active individually; unique people, as we all are at the end of the day. The name that Bakker gave them for the occasion did nothing to change that. In a country where water prevails over earth, wind and fire the term Droog (dry) has an almost magical ring to it that is difficult to put into words. 'Anyone trying to define Droog Design's selection criteria', as Ramakers would later warn the international press, 'will run well and truly aground.'

Droog Design became the visual expression of a prevailing mentality. A virtual collection which even its two 'curators' interpret differently. For Ramakers, the recalcitrant art historian who considers fault lines in tradition more fun than tradition itself, the manifest image - the international zeitgeist in its quintessential form - reigns supreme. Bakker, the conscientious designer who is never satisfied with manifestations purely the result of historical growth and so defiantly starts from scratch every time, prefers to describe it as a visual manifesto; a charter whose clauses are embodied by designs.

In a historic palazzo on the Via Cerva in Milan the body of ideas of both nonconformists was brought into view.[5] Their congenital abhorrence of habit and boredom, their cause-defending role within the design world and all those earlier attempts at reconciliation with indus[...] had now found expression in a make-believe collection of twenty products. T[...] spiritual content, which Ramakers in the past had often vainly sought beneath the straightlaced surface of Dutch design, all at once was there. The hopes and expectations that Bakker had voiced in an interview seven years earlier, had become reality. 'Experiments done in the Netherlands', he said at the time, 'are still too redolent of Memphis. I'm waiting for a sequel to the Italian group ... but then from the northern countries.'[6] During that 32nd Milan fair the existing hegemony was breached. All at once the avant-garde had a new language, purged of jargon, slogans and mottoes, without isms, without dogmas, yet internationally comprehensible. These Dutch forms proved able to communicate universally. 'Their packaging had the intelligence not to obstruct the narrative, much like Sartre's Les Mots,' for Bakker still the most sublime combination of words and that which they make known. Droog Design avant la lettre then. 'Savoir-vivre spirituel', as the French periodical Libération described the Dutch contribution at Milan. 'They tell the most improbable of stories. Fairytales without fairies. Fleeting. They are brilliant in that they arouse the desire to revivify the quotidian in life. Design for them is not a question of taste but an ongoing issue. That makes you feel better. The way a stroll through the flea market does.'[7]

Design had returned to the man in the street. No shock effects, no veiled slogans or punchy epithets. Even the rebellious assemblage of drawers called 'You can't lay down your memories' was too

Tejo Remy, Milk bottle lamp, 1991
27 x 36 cm (length variable), 15 watt overhangs, sand-blasted milk bottles, stainless steel. Manufacturer DMD, Voorburg

The milk bottles hang just above the ground on long cables in a cluster of twelve — three times four rows of bottles, exactly as it is in a Dutch milk crate.

Ed Annink, Multipurpose hook, 1992

13 x 15 cm, soft polyurethane Manufacturer: DMD, Voorburg

'I like products that are rooted in things that already exist, only realized in another material and another size, and in another context.'

poetic to provoke. Ramakers hit the nail on the head when she described the public response to Droog Design as a flash of recognition. Familiar products more likely to raise a smile than a scowl. 'It's a marvellous experience to see that this design, more idea than formgiving, is catching on more with a very broad public than with just the loyal design coterie.'[8]

Back home, with furniture megastores everywhere and little trace of a furniture industry, it became clear that the short-lived intuitive adventure in Milan had been too good to treat as a nine-day's wonder. Droog Design got itself nicely secured in a typically Dutch legal construct, the foundation. An equally important move was to find a producer, one able to bring to fruition prototypes simply clamouring to join in everyday life. Development, Manufacturing, Distribution, DMD for short, took up the challenge in the person of Teake Bulstra.[9] Meanwhile, Ramakers' and Bakker's mania for collecting continued undiminished. A letter weighing machine based on Archimedes' principle, a chair full of holes, a cluster of eighty-five light-bulbs, a copper mixing faucet, flowerbulb packaging made of dried cowdung, socket lights; the motley assortment of products admittedly had much on occasion of a cabinet of curiosities.[10] But the display was never divorced from quotidian existence, and never staid or static. Designs came, designs went. Now and again products were unceremoniously taken out of production. And each and every year, Milan was the rockhard touchstone.

In those early days, Droog Design was firmly linked for no good reason to environmentally sound design: trash designers and their eco-products. Critics accordingly consigned most of the products onto the fashionable dungheap of contemporary design. But Droog has never been an ecological movement, insists Ramakers. Though many of the designers shared the view that more than enough had been designed, their approach was significantly different; why not work with strong archetypes rather than cling to the illusion of the new product? In that sense, recycling, instead of sticking closely to the letter became a process of the mind. Tejo Remy's rag chair is as far from a complaint against the chemical emission from textile factories, as Konings and Bey's bookcase made of paper is from a protest against the unremitting exploitation of the earth's resources.

'Droog Design', exhibition in INTERNOS, Via Capuccio, Milan, April 1996. Exhibition design: OVAL.

One might almost describe it as a philosophical approach, a bending of rigid thinking into a spiritual, intellectual cycle. Just as the absent-minded professor and the simple-minded village idiot are two polarities that might resemble one another in everyday life, so wealth and poverty are interchangeable ideas in Rody Graumans' chandelier. Utter restraint and extravagance. Flea market and museum. Past and future. Within Droog Design these seem to have lost their validity as paradox. Marcel Wanders' stacked lampshades, Gijs Bakker's

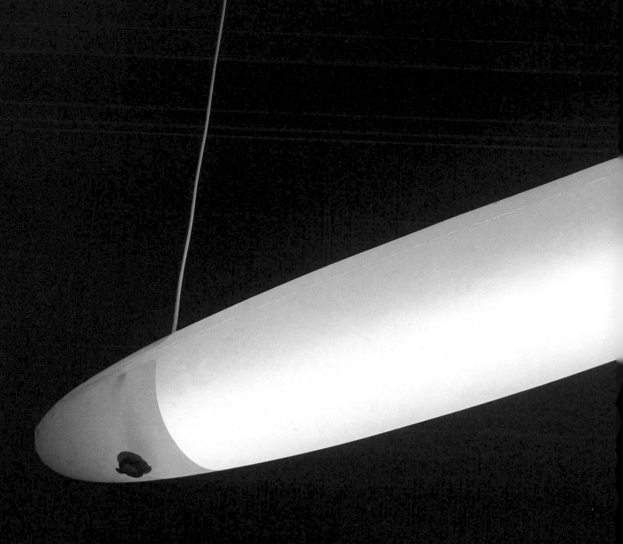

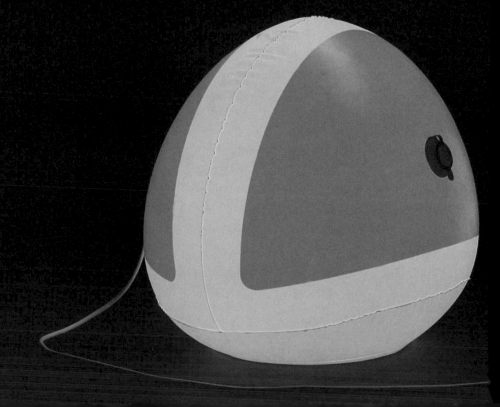

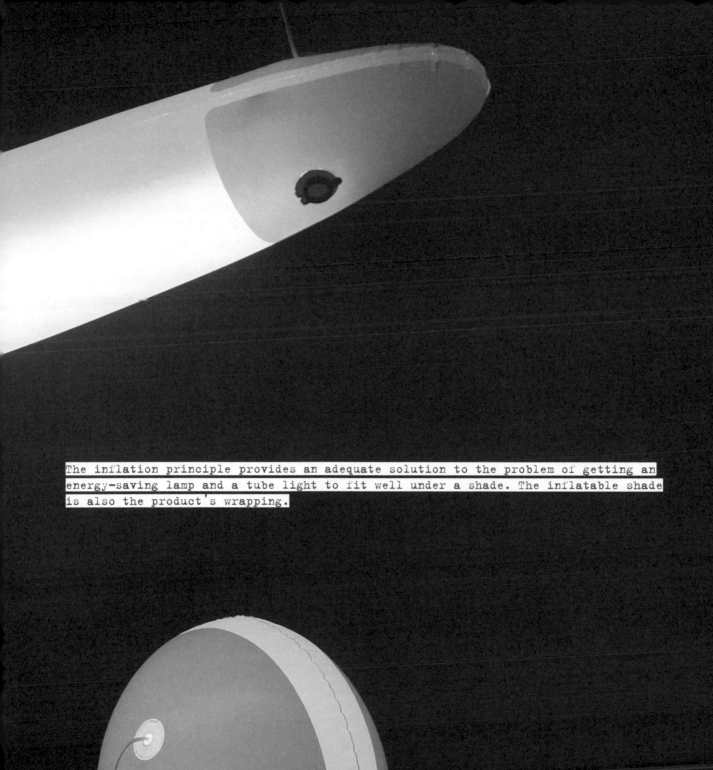

The inflation principle provides an adequate solution to the problem of getting an energy-saving lamp and a tube light to fit well under a shade. The inflatable shade is also the product's wrapping.

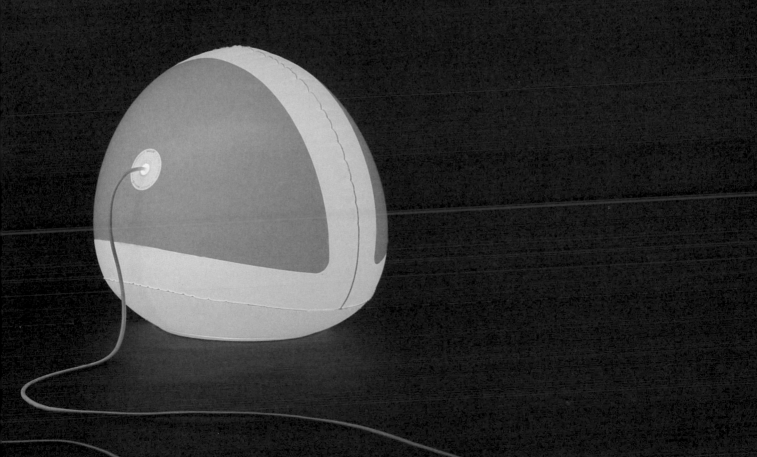

perforated chair - these are Van Gogh's Potato Eaters, but this time armed with silver forks.

Closely linked to the manic fear of being lumped together with a house style, Bakker and Ramakers in time fell prey to an insidious sense of dissatisfaction with the trend that threatened to overtake them. As the Milan successes burgeoned, so the army of epigons yearly swelled its ranks. The rough surface became a neatly fenced-off, smooth-trodden playground full of trampoline floors and fun objects. Droog Design became associated with everything it denounced: a style, a trade, an ideology, an umbrella against the elements...

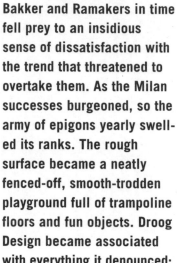

'Dry Bathing', exhibition in Spazio Antonio Colombo, Via Solferino, Milan, April 1997. The 'Dry Bathing' project was organized in collaboration with DMD to develop new ideas for the bathroom. The installation was designed by Ed Annink.

After three years of carefree intuition and fanciful selection it was decided to change course. The curators also became initiators; both out of necessity, and simply because it was in their blood. The free agent's inbuilt fear of boredom prompted them to steer their body of ideas onto a relatively unfamiliar path. In the spring of 1995, Ramakers had already given evidence, in an editorial in Items, of a growing sense of disquiet regarding the day when the rough-hewn low-tech aesthetic and the new adventure of high-tech materials would cross paths. [11] 'We're anxiously awaiting the outcome' were her sentiments at the time. But instead of

Droog Design catalogue, 1994.
Graphic design: Joseph Plateau

waiting she immediately took matters into her own hands. The Aviation and Space Laboratory at the TU Delft threw open its doors to Droog Design. A new experimental future was in the offing. With the arrival of the Dry Tech project, the coherent image strewn during those first years like handfuls of sand across the international design world, all at once took on a transparent coating. Dick van Hoff had shot off in the same direction with his felt washbasin, and Hella Jongerius' rubber vase showed what could happen when 'artisans' exchanged their ivory tower for a plastic laboratory. Dry Tech resumed this thread, albeit one of synthetic fibre. Marcel Wanders macraméd his Knotted Chair from carbon fibre and aramid. Martijn Hoogendijk fused traditional felt with polyurethane and synthetic fibre. Jongerius knitted a glass-fibre lamp. When Droog Design presented their wares last April in Milan for the fifth time, the image was as familiar as before. Yet there was a noticeably different slant to it. The controversy of the early days no longer rested on orange boxes and ragbags. Revolt against sterile perfection and the mechanical self-image of man had pushed on into the lion's den, where the laws of technique and function are all-powerful. However, the clean, state-of-the-art space-age world of Delft was only the beginning. Shortly after, Droog Design would smash to smithereens the traditional image of the Rosenthal porcelain factory at Selb in Germany. Uninhibited by neither the slightest knowledge of the subject nor by the vaguest sense of history, five designers led by Gijs Bakker quite literally saturated the fragile milk-white material with their own irony. [12] Bakker made no bones about confronting such well-loved teapot classics as the 'Maria' and the 'Accent' with their own frumpishness. It was Rosenthal itself that had invited this not inconsiderable crack in the porcelain tradition. The proverbial bull had been welcomed into the china shop with open arms.

Dry Tech, Droog Design for Rosenthal and Dry Bathing[13] may have blazed new trails, but had led also to a certain closeness, the very group sense and style thinking that Ramakers and Bakker sought to avoid. 'And yet', admitted Bakker, 'those projects were necessary to safeguard our ideas.' His words have a moralistic undertone that Ramakers acknowledges wholeheartedly. 'Each show, each venture articulates a vision. In our own way, as we want to bring out the essence.' No style then, just a coherent image, though one that clings the way sand does.

Five years after the event, the future of this phenomenon is as rhapsodic and unpredictable as ever. The magic sound that the indefinable word 'droog' has for other countries, has lost nothing of its enchantment. Here in the Netherlands recognition took a more cramped, possessive form. The rational Dutchman simply has little affinity, not to say great difficulty, with anything he cannot immediately put a name to. Soon after the birth of Droog Design, Dutch universities already started to analyse the phenomenon that had taken international opinion so forcibly by storm. The scepticism usually found among academics regarding national character and zeitgeist, was pushed aside on this occasion. But even

an exhaustive and bulky doctoral thesis failed to penetrate to the prime meat of Droog Design. It was evidently hard work getting the sum of the parts to add up right. [14]

More 'patrons' entered the arena. In 1997 the Centraal Museum in Utrecht bought up the complete collection 1993-1996. All the designs taken into the care of Droog Design since that first bracing stroll through the flea market, were dragged unceremoniously into the museum. And strictly speaking the virtual collection ceased to exist forthwith. 'Perhaps it would have been better if we were dead and buried,' was Bakker and Ramakers's laconic reaction to this manic show of collecting by real-life curators. But they know better than anyone else that at the end of the day, the true coup de grâce will be a much more impressive and grander affair, and that only time can make that thrust.

Fashion show 'Le Cri Néerlandais' during the opening of the exhibition 'Droog Design' in INTERNOS - DONNA ELISSA, Milan, 1995.

Notes

1   Interview with Gijs Bakker, Amsterdam 3 June 1997.
2   Ron Kaal, 'The absolute form', in Items 7, 1995, p. 35.
3   Michel van Tongeren, 'Post-Paradise',
     in Vormberichten 6, 1996, p. 23.
4   Jaap Huisman, 'Onverbiddelijke terugkeer naar de
     eenvoud', in de Volkskrant 3-2-1995.
5   The space was rented from Pastoe furniture manufacturers.
6   Ella Reitsma, 'Opvattingen over industriële vormgeving',
     in Vrij Nederland, 22-2-1986, p. 9.
7   Brigitte Ollier, 'Les sept clés du prêt-a-meubler', in
     Libération, 30-4/2-5-1993, pp. 41, 42.
8   Interview with Renny Ramakers, The Hague,
     13 May 1997.
9   DMD, domiciled in Voorburg, now have fifteen designs by
     Droog Design in production.
10   Michael Horsham, 'What is Droog?', in Blueprint, October
     1996, p. 53.
11   Renny Ramakers, Items 4, 1995, p. 6.

dmd-62

Peter van der Jagt, Doorbell 'Bottoms Up', 1994

25 x 9 x... cm, stainless steel, crystal glass, electromagnet. Manufacturer: DMD, Voorburg

'What we know as a doorbell is a square box that strangely enough says nothing about what a doorbell really is: an appliance consisting of an electromagnet, a hammer and two sound sources, announcing the arrival of guests. Crystal glasses make a pleasant sound, indeed they symbolize sound. This bell announces guests with a musical toast.'

12   The first contact between Rosenthal and Droog Design
     was made in April 1996 during the Milan fair. Those who
     took part in the experiment were Gijs Bakker, Dick van
     Hoff, Hella Jongerius, Arnout Visser and Marcel Wanders.
     The initial results were made public in April 1997 in the
     Rosenthal showroom at Corso Mattiotti during the Milan
     furniture fair.
13   'Dry Bathing'. A number of designers were commissioned
     to develop new ideas for bathrooms in collaboration with
     DMD. Hella Jongerius, Arnout Visser, Peter van der Jagt,
     Erik Jan Kwakkel and Roland Buschmann were those who
     worked on the project.
14   Miranda Berden, Droog Design, doctoral thesis in
     the History of Art at the Rijksuniversiteit Leiden, March
     1007.

Group picture taken for the Dutch magazine
Eigen Huis & Interieur, 1995.

Above from left to right:
Eibert Draisma, Edith Verhoeven, Martijn Hoogendijk,
Arnout Visser, Ed Annink, Henk Stallinga.
Standing from left to right:
Gijs Bakker, Renny Ramakers, Tejo Remy, Jan Konings,
Teake Bulstra, Djoke de Jong, Marcel Wanders,
Richard Hutten.
Sitting in the foreground from left to right:
Gert Jan Leusink, Rody Graumans, Hella Jongerius.

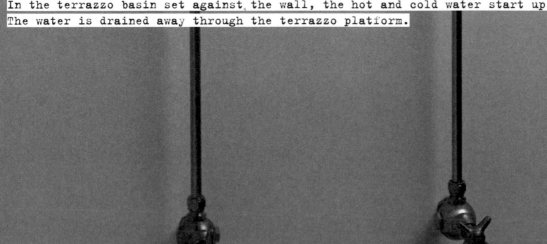

In the terrazzo basin set against the wall, the hot and cold water start up a 'waterfall'.
The water is drained away through the terrazzo platform.

'In "Set up shades" it's not recycling the material or the ready-made aspect that interests me. What does is the reuse of the archetype, the recycling of the idea. This because I want to make products that are well-worn favourites even when being first introduced.'

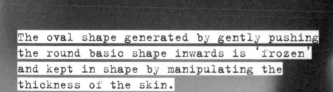

The oval shape generated by gently pushing
the round basic shape inwards is 'frozen'
and kept in shape by manipulating the
thickness of the skin.

Konings & Bey, Wardrobe / Konings & Bey, Hanging Wardrobe, 1990

50 x 50 x 200 cm, aluminium, cotton / 60 x 60 x 200 cm, aluminium, cotton Not in production

'We wanted to make the two wardrobes out of the materials of the things you put in them. The one in which clothes are lain flat, has shelves and an outer wrapping of knitted cotton; the hanging wardrobe is closed off with hanging cotton sheets.'

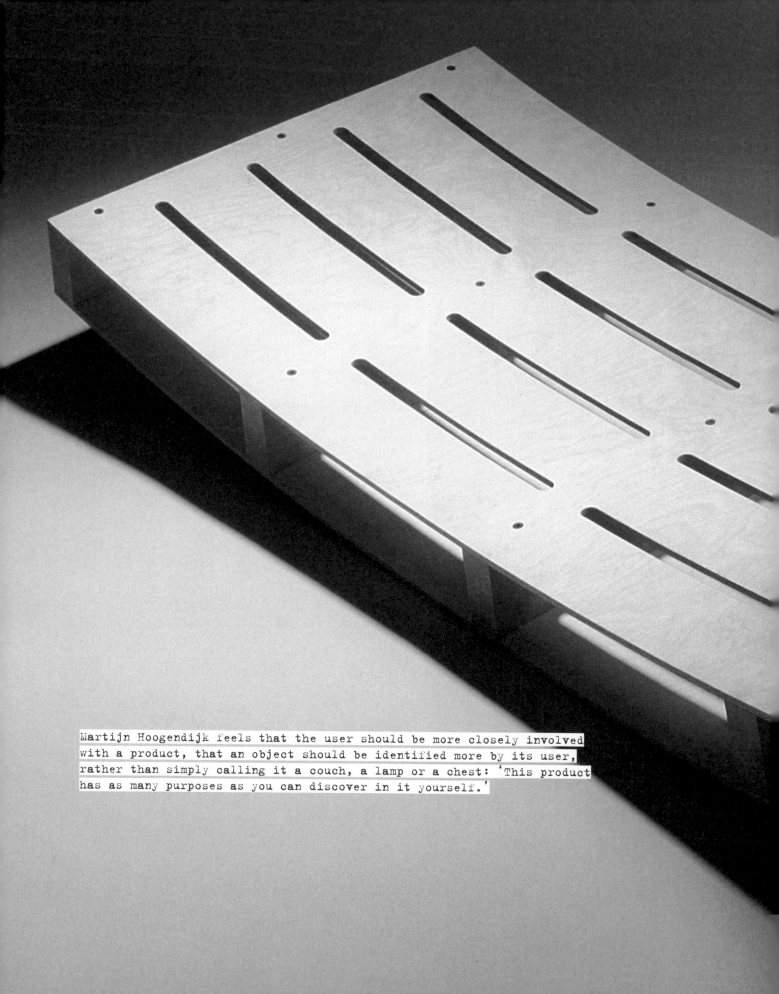

Martijn Hoogendijk feels that the user should be more closely involved with a product, that an object should be identified more by its user, rather than simply calling it a couch, a lamp or a chest: 'This product has as many purposes as you can discover in it yourself.'

Martijn Hoogendijk, **Pallet**, 1993
170 x 68 x 12 cm, beechwood Manufacturer: Martijn Hoogendijk

The material used fits the contents: textile. It is a
knitted fabric that has been partly fixed by
polyurethane resin, which gives it body and strength.
The non-impregnated end is tied up and turned inwards in
a casual manner, to allow the basket to breathe.

A wall socket and lamp in one.

Roland Buschmann, **Toothbrush mirror,** 1995

30 x 42 cm, wire, reflecting glass   Manufacturer: DMD, Voorburg

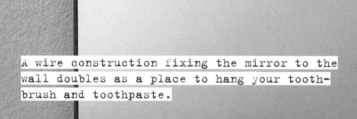

A wire construction fixing the mirror to the
wall doubles as a place to hang your toothbrush and toothpaste.

Frank Tjepkema, Artificial Bloom Construction set, 1996
21 x 30 cm, plastic, cardboard Manufacturer: Present Time, Almere

artificial
Bloom

All the components you need to create your genuine artificial flower.

Happy birthday ☐
Congratulations ☐
Forever yours ☐
I love you ☐
Baby *BLOOM* ☐
Let's meet again ☐
.... ☐

Ⓟ t
(Droog Design) for

design Frank Tjepkema

This steel cabinet – including the hinges and symbols referring to use – is held together by magnets. Nothing has been constructed.

Droog
Activit

Design
es

1995 saw the 'Dry Tech' project set up in collaboration with the
Aviation and Space Laboratory of Delft University of Technology,
the aim being to combine rough-and-ready low-tech aesthetics
with high-tech materials. The designers set to work along
artisanal and intuitive lines. In 1996 the first results were
presented in Milan: Hella Jongerius's 'Knitted lamp',
Marcel Wanders's 'Knotted chair' and Martijn Hoogendijk's 'Wave'.
Dry Tech II was shown in Milan in April 1997: Konings & Bey's
'Kokon' furniture, Hella Jongerius's 'wrap stools' and
Marcel Wanders's 'lace tables'.

Hoogendijk glaze-melted the traditional felt with polyurethane
and polyester fibres.

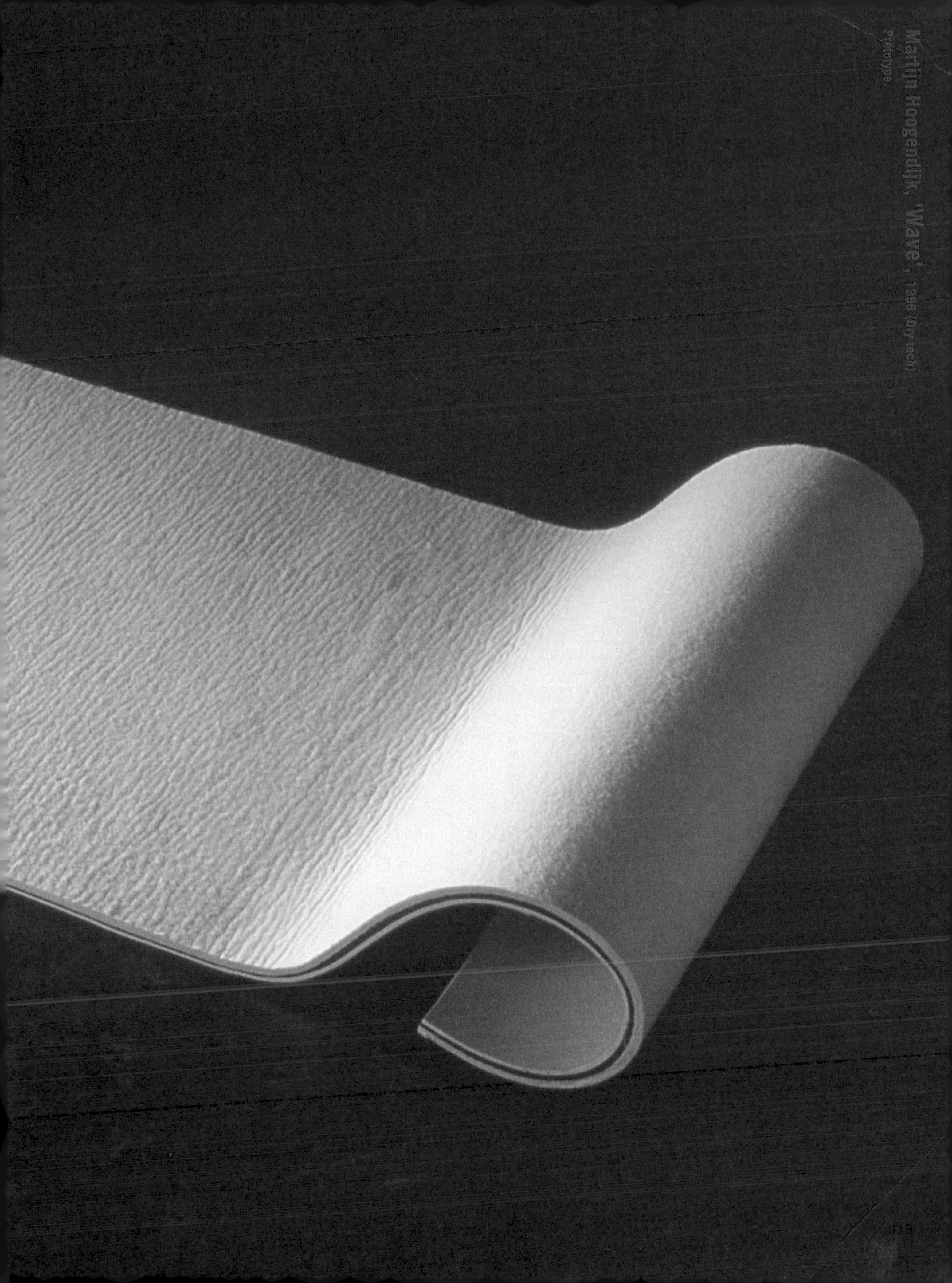

Martijn Hoogendijk, 'Wave', 1996 (Dry tech)
Prototype.

A transparent series of tables was made
by hardening Swiss lace with resin.

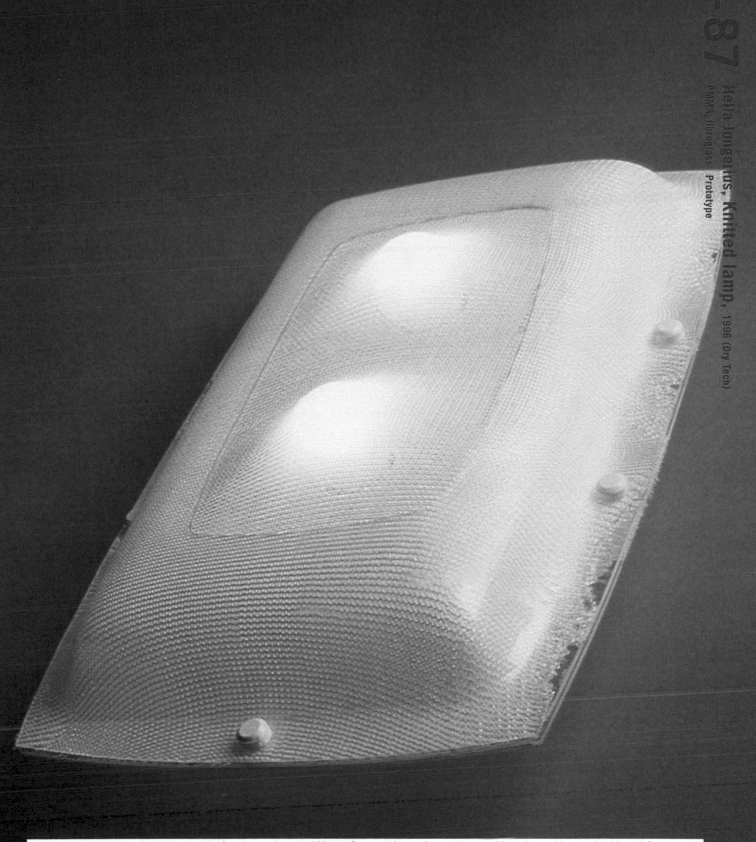

Hella Jongerius knitted a cloth out of fibreglass threads, strengthening it on both sides with perspex. This cloth was then ready to receive a number of lamp bulbs. The bulbs press through the knitted fibreglass, so that the cloth follows the shape of the bulbs.

Hella Jongerius, 'Wrap stools', 1997 (Dry Tech)
Prototype.

The stools have been coiled at random from different fibres: yellow aramid
or peacock-blue Rigid-Rod polymer M5.

Macramé meets high-tech. This light-weight chair is born of a marriage between handicraft and industrial technology. The rope made of an aramid braid and carbon centre is knotted into the shape of a chair. Then the slack texture is impregnated with epoxy and hung in a frame to harden. Gravity creates the final shape.

These products have been wrapped in an elastic synthetic fibre with the help of a 'spiderweb technique'. With this technique, one that is used in aviation, it is possible to cover open parts. The material shrinks round a skeleton and forms a smooth elastic skin. The chairs are the first in a series of products. The 'skeleton' is a well-known chair, with the elastic skin adding an entirely new appearance. By cross-breeding and grafting, products and functions of a different nature can merge and develop into new products.

Konings & Bey, 'Kokon' furniture, 1997 (Dry Tech)

PVC Coating, existing furniture Prototype

Droog De
Rosenth.

esign for
al

During the Milan show of April 1996 Droog Design was approached by the well-known German porcelain factory of Rosenthal to take part in an experimental project. Droog developed various ideas with regard to use, texture, colour and the production process, ideas which Rosenthal subsequently realized. The results were presented at the Rosenthal showroom in Milan in April 1997. In the following August the products were shown at the 'Tendence' trade fair in Frankfurt. Many now belong to the Droog collection.

Dick van Hoff, Porcelain lamp, 1997
(Droog Design for Rosenthal) Porcelain, metal Prototype

This lamp was born out of
dissatisfaction with the
existing techniques, in this
case the usual dichotomy of
fitting and shade. In this
design the porcelain fitting
literally melts into the shade,
which is also made of porcelain.

Visualizing insulation has been the starting point of a series of double-walled products. The inner shape is glazed, the outer is not. In the firing process, the unglazed outer shape melts together with the glazed inner shape.

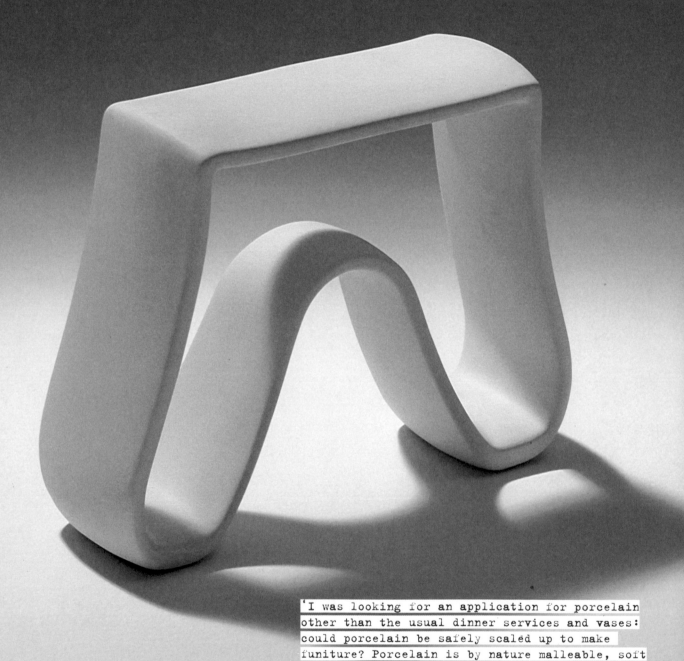

'I was looking for an application for porcelain other than the usual dinner services and vases: could porcelain be safely scaled up to make funiture? Porcelain is by nature malleable, soft and warm. It's only in the firing process that it gets rigid, hard and cold. I wanted the stool to express the true nature of the material.'

A sponge is dipped in fluid porcelain clay. After drying, the porcelain-impregnated sponge is burnt in an oven. The sponge disappears entirely and the porcelain adapts perfectly to its shape. In this way porcelain products can be created without the use of moulds.

Marcel Wanders, Eggshell vase, 1997 (Droog Design for Rosenthal),
Porcelain, prototype.

The shape was determined by stuffing rubber condoms with hard boiled eggs.

A cosy has been knitted round the Maria coffeepot, a classic item in the
Rosenthal collection. The knitted part integrated with the porcelain
during the glazing process.

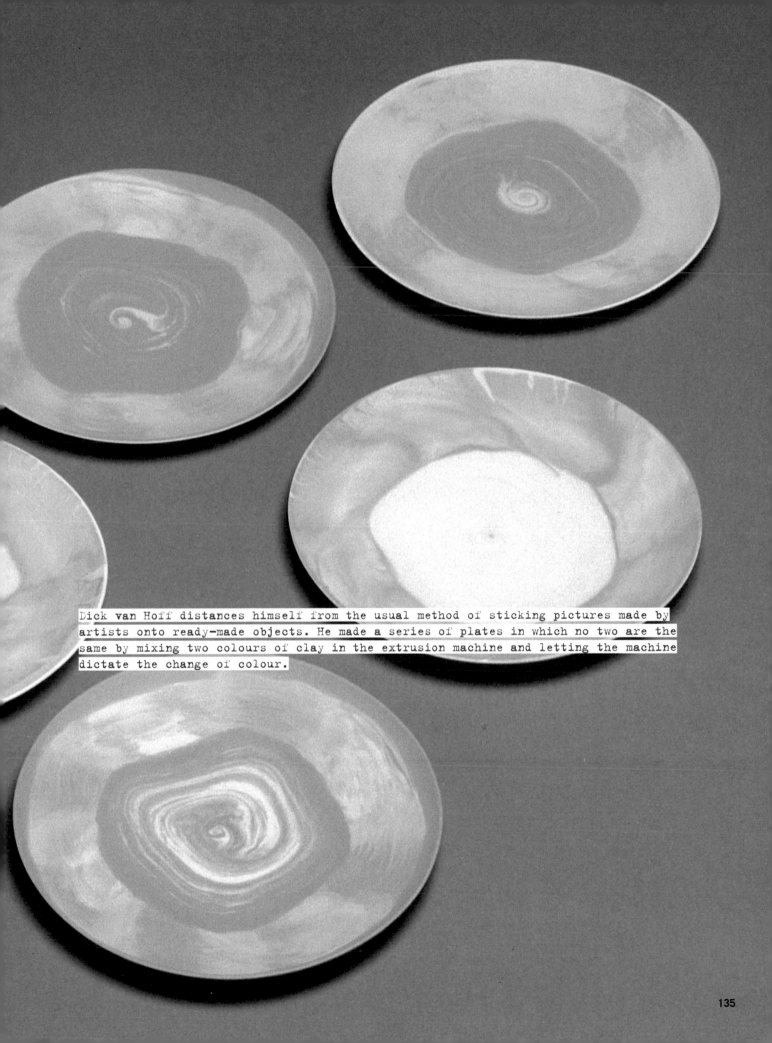

Dick van Hoff distances himself from the usual method of sticking pictures made by artists onto ready-made objects. He made a series of plates in which no two are the same by mixing two colours of clay in the extrusion machine and letting the machine dictate the change of colour.

igh-tech 'Accent', 1997

(...senthal) Porcelain, Alumina-Boria-Silica fibres   Prototype

The latest developments in the field of flexible fibres that can take extremely high temperatures, make it possible for traditional products to embark on a whole new life. The handle of the 'Accent' teapot, a classic item in the Rosenthal collection, has now been made of twined ceramic fibre glaze-melted to the pot.

A classical labyrinth pattern of iron oxide glaze has been added to the bottom
of existing plates. Because of the decoration it is possible to heat a pile of
plates in the microwave: the bottom of the plates stays warm for some time,
while the edges stay cool.

Chronology

1993

28 February
'Een middag gewoon doen', Paradiso, Amsterdam This exhibition was organized by Renny Ramakers following a number of minor shows collectively entitled 'Things look that way now' at Interieur 92, Kortrijk, Belgium, and at Musis Sacrum in Arnhem, in October and December 1992 respectively.

20 - 25 April
'Pastoe & Droog Design', exhibition at Via Cerva 14, Milan, during the International Furniture Fair, in association with the Nederlands Vormgevingsinstituut. Andrea Branzi opened the show.

The collaboration between Droog Design and the company DMD begins. DMD develops part of the Droog Design collection for production and builds up an international network of producers and distributors.

1994

28 February
Droog Design Foundation established.

14 January - 10 April
Participation in 'Design aus den Niederlanden', exhibition in Museum für Angewandte Kunst in Cologne.

11 - 17 April
'Droog Design', exhibition in gallery INTERNOS-DONNA ELISSA, Via Bernadino Luini 7, Milan, during the International Furniture Fair, in association with the Nederlands Vormgevingsinstituut. Ed Annink designed the exhibition, which was accompanied by a modest catalogue.

1995

17 - 22 January
'Droog Design & DMD', show held at Chapel Design Center, Jülicher Strasse 26, Cologne, during the International Furniture Fair.

16 March - 17 May
Droog takes part in the exhibition 'Die Kunst und das schöne Ding'. Jean Nouvel presents selected products from the International Design Yearbook 1995, Museum Weserburg, Bremen, Germany.

7 - 11 April
'Droog Design by DMD', exhibition in gallery INTERNOS-DONNA ELISSA, Via Bernadino Luini 7, Milan, during the International Furniture Fair, in association with the Nederlands Vormgevingsinstituut. Ed Annink designed the exhibition. During the opening the Nederlands Vormgevingsinstituut held a fashion show by 'Le Cri Nëerlandais'.

22 - 26 September
Droog takes part in 'ECO WAY', an exhibition on ecological design in the furniture industry, compiled by Serena Omodeo and Cristina Morozzi, 'Abitare il Tempo', Verona, Italy.

29 October
Droog contributes to the Dutch garden café in the Museum of Modern Art, New York.

7 November 1995 - 4 January 1996
Droog contributes to 'Mentalitäten. Niederlandisches Design', products nominated for the Designprijs Rotterdam 1993-1995, Securitas Galerie, Bremen, Germany.

2 December 1995 - 28 January 1996
Exhibition 'Droog Design' in the Kunsthal, Rotterdam. The show was designed by Konings & Bey in association with Roelof Mulder.

18 December 1995 - 13 January 1996
Droog takes part in the opening exhibition of Perigot Entreprises in the Carroussel du Louvre, Paris.

1996

15 - 19 January
'Droog Design', exhibition in Andrea Leenarts gallery, Cologne, Germany, during the International Furniture Fair.

5 February - 7 April
Droog contributes to the exhibition 'Design Now! design from the Netherlands', organized by the Products of Imagination foundation in the Centre de design de l'UQUAM, Montréal, Canada.

18 - 22 April
'Droog Design. Plastics new treat' and 'Droog Design by DMD', two shows at INTERNOS gallery, Via Capucci 21a, Milan, during the International Furniture Fair. Exhibition design by OVAL.

April - June
Droog takes part in the exhibition 'Design im Wandel'. Alessandro Mendini's selection from the International Design Yearbook 1996, Übersee Museum, Bremen, Germany.

5 May - 2 June 1996
Droog contributes to Mentalitäten. Niederländisches Design, products nominated for the Designprijs Rotterdam 1993-1996, Designzentrum, Stuttgart, Germany.

27 June - 4 November
Droog contributes to the exhibition 'Thresholds; Contemporary Design from The Netherlands' in the Museum of Modern Art, New York.

29 November - 28 December
Exhibition 'Droog Design', Sentou Galerie, Paris.

November - March 1997
Droog takes part in the opening exhibition of Material ConneXion, Material Innovation Gallery, New York.

1997

14 - 19 January
'Droog Design', presentation in Galerie Ulrich Fiedler, Lindenstraase 19, Cologne, during the International Furniture Fair.

21 January - 15 February
Droog takes part in the exhibition 'Handmade in the Benelux' In The Gallery in Cork Street, 28 Cork Street, London.

19 February - 3 October
Droog contributes to the exhibition
'Not so simple' in the Victoria & Albert Museum, London.

21 March - 27 April
Exhibition 'Droog Design' in Taideteollisuusmuseo in Helsinki, Finland.

22 - 24 March
Droog takes part in the limited competition 'Pirelli Design per il fianco di "pneumatico per autocarro"'. The results are published in a numbered catalogue (edition of 1000) by Edizione Pirelli Spa, Naples, March 1996.

24 March
The Centraal Museum, Utrecht, buys the Droog Design collection 1993-1996.

9 - 14 April
'Droog Design' presentations during the International Furniture Fair in Milan.
'Dry Bathing' (new ideas for the bathroom) and 'Dry Tech II' (a new series of low-high-tech products) in Spazio Solferino, Via Solferino 44. Ed Annink designed the show. 'Droog Design for Rosenthal', presentation in Rosenthal Studio Haus, Corso Matteotti 8, Milan. Marcel Wanders designed the show. 'Droog Design by DMD' presentation at DOVETUSAI, Via Sannio 24, Milan.

22 April
'Prix d'Excellence de la maison 1997' for 'the spirit of the collection Droog Design', awarded in Paris by the magazine Marie Claire.

23 May - 22 June
'Droog Design. Zeitgenössisches Design aus den Niederlanden', exhibition in the Kulturbrauerei, Galerie im Pferdestall, Knaackstrasse 97, Berlin.

6 June - 28 September
Droog contributes to the exhibition 'Design mit Zukunft'. Philippe Starck's selection from the International Design Yearbook 1997, Focke Museum, Bremen, Germany.

4 July - 17 August
Exhibition 'Droog Design' in the Centraal Museum, Utrecht.

23 - 28 August
Exhibition 'Droog Design for Rosenthal' at the Tendence fair in Frankfurt, Germany.

14 September - 30 November
Droog Design takes part in the exhibition 'Mutant Materials in Contemporary Design' at the Groninger Museum, Groningen. The exhibition was curated by Paola Antonelli, Associate Curator at the Department of Design and Architecture, the Museum of Modern Art, New York.

16 September - 19 October
Exhibition 'Droog Design' in Stilwerk, Hamburg, Germany.

24 October - 7 December
Exhibition 'Droog Design' at ACC Galerie, Weimar, Germany.

Acknowledgements

This book has been made possible by the generous support of the Mondriaan Foundation
and the Prins Bernhard Fonds.
Editing by Renny Ramakers and Gijs Bakker
Texts by Paola Antonelli, Renny Ramakers, Yvonne Brentjens
Translation into English by John Kirkpatrick
Graphic Design by Roelof Mulder in association with Annemarie van Pruyssen
Photography collection Droog Design by Bob Goedewagen, Richard Hutten, Rene Koster,
Jannes Linders, Marsel Loermans, Hans van der Mars, Ernst Moritz, Nienke Terpstra,
F. Tjepkema. Photography Dutch landscapes by ANP
Printed by Snoeck Ducaju, Gent
© 1998 The authors and 010 Publishers / www.archined.nl/010
ISBN 90 6450 301 X

With thanks to Christine de Baan, Ed van Hinte, Peter Hopman, Wim Pijbes, Saskia Wijne and Ingeborg de Wolff for
their help and advice during the making of this book, and to Miranda Berden for allowing access to her doctoral thesis
in the History of Art, devoted to Droog Design, when compiling the captions to the illustrated products.